Amanda Jackson
Peirong Lin (Ed.)

**Co-workers and co-leaders
Women and men partnering for God's work**

The WEA Global Issues Series

Editors:

Thomas Schirrmacher
Secretary General, World Evangelical Alliance

Bishop Efraim Tendero, Philippines
Global Ambassador of World Evangelical Alliance

Volumes:

1. Thomas K. Johnson – Human Rights
2. Christine Schirrmacher – The Islamic View of Major Christian Teachings
3. Thomas Schirrmacher – May a Christian Go to Court?
4. Christine Schirrmacher – Islam and Society
5. Thomas Schirrmacher – The Persecution of Christians Concerns Us All
6. Christine Schirrmacher – Islam – An Introduction
7. Thomas K. Johnson – What Difference does the Trinity Make
8. Thomas Schirrmacher – Racism
9. Christof Sauer (ed.) – Bad Urach Statement
10. Christine Schirrmacher – The Sharia: Law and Order in Islam
11. Ken Gnanakan – Responsible Stewardship of God's Creation
12. Thomas Schirrmacher – Human Trafficking
13. Thomas Schirrmacher – Ethics of Leadership
14. Thomas Schirrmacher – Fundamentalism
15. Thomas Schirrmacher – Human Rights – Promise and Reality
16. Christine Schirrmacher – Political Islam – When Faith Turns Out to Be Politics
17. Thomas Schirrmacher, Thomas K. Johnson – Creation Care and Loving our Neighbors: Studies in Environmental Ethics
18. Thomas K. Johnson (Ed.) – Global Declarations on Freedom of Religion or Belief and Human Rights
19. Thomas Schirrmacher, David Schirrmacher – Corruption
20. Christine Schirrmacher, Thomas Schirrmacher – The Oppression of Women: Violence – Exploitation – Poverty
21. Christine Schirrmacher – Islam and Democracy
22. Amanda Jackson, Peirong Lin (Ed.) – Co-workers and co-leaders Women and men partnering for God's work

"The WEA Global Issues Series is designed to provide thoughtful, practical, and biblical insights from an Evangelical Christian perspective into some of the greatest challenges we face in the world. I trust you will find this volume enriching and helpful in your life and Kingdom service."

Amanda Jackson
Peirong Lin (Ed.)

Co-workers and co-leaders
Women and men partnering for God's work

Verlag für Kultur und Wissenschaft
Culture and Science Publ.
Dr. Thomas Schirrmacher
Bonn 2021

World Evangelical Alliance
Church Street Station, P.O. Box 3402
New York, NY 10008-3402 U.S.A.
Phone +[1] 212-233-3046
Fax +[1] 646-957-9218
www.worldevangelicals.org / wea@worldea.org

While this volume does not represent an "official" position of the World Evangelical Alliance we are distributing it to promote further serious study and reflection.

International Institute for Religious Freedom
of the World Evangelical Alliance
www.iirf.eu / info@iirf.eu

Friedrichstr. 38	PO Box 1336	32, Ebenezer Place	Setor Bancário Sul,
2nd Floor	Sun Valley 7985	Dehiwela	QD 02, LT 15,
53111 Bonn	Cape Town	(Colombo)	BL E, Room 601
Germany	South Africa	Sri Lanka	Brasilia, Brazil

© Copyright 2021 by
Verlag für Kultur und Wissenschaft Prof. Schirrmacher
UG (haftungsbeschränkt)
Amtsgericht Bonn HRB 20699 / Börsenverein 97356
Geschäftsführer: Prof. Dr. theol. Dr. phil. Thomas Schirrmacher
Friedrichstraße 38, 53111 Bonn, Germany
Fax +49 / 228 / 9650389
www.vkwonline.com / info@vkwonline.com

ISBN 978-3-86269-221-7 / ISSN 1867-7320

Cover: © Good Studio / Adobe Stock

Printed in Germany
Cover design:
Catriona Baker / HCB Verlagsservice Beese
Production:
CPI Books / Buch Bücher.de GmbH, 96158 Birkach
www.cpi-print.de / info.birkach@cpi-print.de
Publisher's Distribution:
www.vkwonline.com
Individual sales: via Amazon or http://wipfandstock.com

The WEA Global Issues Series is sponsored by:
Gebende Hände gGmbH / Giving Hands International
Baumschulallee 3a • 53115 Bonn, Germany • www.giving-hands.de
Martin Bucer Seminary
European Theological School and Research Institutes
Bonn – Delhi – Helsinki – Istanbul –Prague – São Paulo – Tirana – Zurich
www.bucer.org

Contents

Foreword 7

Introduction 9

The Call to Discipleship: Difficult Partnerships 13
    Rosalee Velloso Ewell

Overlooked Women in the Bible 19
    Mary Evans

Women Participating as Equal Partners in the Mission of God 25
    Peirong Lin

Galatians 3:28: a Vision for Partnership 35
    Samuel Oluwatosin Okanlawon

More than Kindness – Jesus' Encounters with Women 47
    Amanda Jackson

Women and Men and Ministry in First-Century Churches 59
    Margaret Mowczko

Lessons from History: how Culture can Distort Interpretation of Scripture 75
    Andrew Bartlett

Stories Today 89

Partnership Intended by God 91
    Reverends Gabriel & Jeanette Salguero

Impact: Partnership in God between Husband and Wife 95
    Florence Muindi

Unity, To Let the World Know! 97
    Leslie and Chad Segraves

Working with Men and Women Takes More than a Smile 101
    Evi Rodemann

Men and Women Co-Working for God's Kingdom 105
  Menchit Wong

Life in Partnership 109
  Emma and Andy Dipper

Singleness and Marriage 113
  Alison Guinness

Partnering as a Single Woman 117
  Amy Summerfield

Paving the Way for Other Women 121
  Madleine Sara

The Journey of Learning 125

A Final Word: Let Us Love One Another and Finish Well 127
  Jay Matenga

Actions we can Take 139

Call to All Christians 141

Other Resources 145

Scripture Index 149

Biographies 153

Foreword

This book presents different perspectives on men and women, in partnership, participating in the *missio Dei*. As Evangelicals, we believe in the good news of Jesus Christ, the son of God, who came to reconcile us to God. He continues to send disciples today.

Whoever comes to believe in God and becomes a Christian receives the power of the Holy Spirit, who gives gifts to enable her or him to actively participate in the *missio Dei*. These gifts are not gender specific: it is God himself who determines who has which gifts and tasks in the church and in mission.

Throughout my Christian ministry, I have worked with women according to their gifts. I have also actively supported women in exercising their gifts, including my wife and daughter. My wife is my best friend and we have a deep respect for each other. We are partners in all ways: we have raised a family, worked and travelled together. When I have something to talk about, I'm always most interested in discussing it with her, my best friend.

Recently, we authored a short book about the oppression of women, highlighting the very real plight of many women today.[1] Women suffer disproportionately from poverty and lack of opportunity. Violence against women continues to be one of the most widespread, persistent and devastating human rights violations in our world and women continue to be sexually exploited.

The WEA has endorsed the "Call to all Christians", developed during the recent "Rise in Strength" consultation for women in international Christian leadership. This call asked for recognition of the plight of women, but also offering hope for the ways the Church can follow Jesus' example in transforming relationships between men and women. I hope that this book helps to inspire all Christians to work together for equal opportunity, equality in ministry according to gifting and for recognition of the very real contribution women make as we pray "your kingdom come."

Thomas Schirrmacher, WEA General Secretary, Spring 2021

---

[1] Christine Schirrmacher and Thomas Schirrmacher, *The Oppression of Women: Violence - Exploitation - Poverty*, 2020, Verlag für Kultur und Wissenschaft.

Introduction

Imagine if men and women could contribute equally to serving and leading the Church. How much stronger and healthier the kingdom of God might be.

This book explores what healthy partnerships can look like in different contexts and how we can overcome barriers of tradition or misunderstanding that hinder us.

Unfortunately, division over interpretations of God's word – the Word that we all want to value – has led to fractious disagreement over the roles and responsibilities of women and men in Christian contexts. These disputes affect the most important human relationships – marriage, family, and working together as God's people. They have limited women from fulfilling their spiritual calling and also trapped men into a limited view of leadership.

We acknowledge that all of us have our blinkers when it comes to this subject. We can all be guilty of quoting our favourite verses to justify our 'truth', so in this book we wanted to overcome fears, doubts and judgements so that we are all better equipped to have strong ministries and a new generation of creative leaders, not because society says so, but because it is God's design. Maybe you find some of the debate about gender in secular society confusing so we have avoided using words that spark strong reactions like feminism or hegemony, or 'religious' terms like egalitarianism or complementarianism (and not just because they are hard to spell!)

This is an accessible book – we have deliberately eschewed being too academic, but we still aim to be intelligent, meticulous and engaging. We want this book to be read in Bible colleges, in home groups across continents, by preachers, teachers, administrators, mission practitioners and parents. Our contributors represent thirteen different nations and nine different languages – that is quite some cultural and church mix!

And we want to be practical, so we have included questions and reflection points at the end of each chapter.

Beginning from the Bible

Our starting point is the Bible and we have gathered seven respected writers to explore texts closely in ways that are creative as well as scholarly. Rosalee Ewell invites us to view the Bible narrative with fresh eyes – to have the big picture of God's character and purposes – to see how God chooses us to work with Him and each other. She posits that Christians have often made the story into one of difference, but that God unites and restores.

For Mary Evans, the narratives about 'forgotten' women reveal God's character in ways we don't find in the Law or the prophets. Her compelling thesis looks at several stories that may be unfamiliar to even seasoned Bible readers: they reveal how cultural norms are never a barrier for God.

Peirong Lin also starts with stories. She traces the narrative of the mission of God through partnership which is rooted in the creation story of Genesis 1-3. It outlines the perspectives of a woman from creation to fall, then redemption.

Look for the careful exegesis of Samuel Oluwatosin Okanlawon on some of the debated passages about women and men in the light of Galatians 3:28, "There is neither male nor female." His arguments are strongly put – maybe it is medicine we all need!

Amanda Jackson traces key encounters Jesus had with women, encounters that were often counter-cultural. His kindness and care are easy to see but we have not always noticed his willingness to teach women and challenge them intellectually.

Marg Mowzcko's walk through the experience of the early church is effortlessly scholarly – how women were involved and what Paul's letters reveal about family and church life for early believers, and us.

Andrew Bartlett's chapter gives us pause for thought as he explores how cultural attitudes to women have crept into interpretation of the Bible through the centuries, limiting their contributions and denying them access to use their gifting.

Moving to examples of today

We have included real life stories – eight personal insights introduced by Gabriel and Jeanette Salguero who have over 20 years' experience being co-leaders in the Church. Their humour and graciousness, and their stand for justice shines in their piece. The stories from women and men of different ages and situations will entertain with their insights. Look out for some of the barriers that they have overcome – they point to big questions about the behaviour and attitudes of Christian leaders – the good and the ugly.

The book finishes on the high point of Jay Matenga's thoughtful analysis of ways forward based on God's radical design for all sorts of relationships. At this time when fresh expressions of churches, many led by women, are forming in many parts of the world, it is more important than ever that we understand God's heart and direction. We want to love one another, and finish well.

The 'Call to All Christians'[2] (printed in the Resources section), has been endorsed by Christian leaders in the World Evangelical Alliance and the Lausanne Movement. It asks "men and women of the global Church to act so that women, men, girls and boys can embrace their spiritual giftings to strengthen the work of the Church, and Her witness to the glory of God." Partnership and mutual encouragement are the way God chooses to work (Father, Son and Holy Spirit). This book has the bold dream to see men and women working and leading together in harmony to demonstrate God to our messy, broken world.

Editors
Amanda Jackson
Peirong Lin

---

[2] The Call to All Christians was written in 2019 by a group of 60 women leaders who gathered in Amsterdam to explore what God is saying to Christians about women and girls, men and boys. The Call is available in 10 languages at www.risein strength.net/download-the-call It follows on from The Lausanne Cape Town Commitment of 2010, which stated, "All of us are responsible to enable all God's people to exercise all the gifts that God has given for all areas of service to which god calls the Church" (p67). The Cape Town Commitment is available in many languages at https://bit.ly/36YNom3.

The Call to Discipleship: Difficult Partnerships

Rosalee Velloso Ewell

Ministry belonging to God

There is a danger that a book or conversation about women and men in partnership in Christian ministry can get highjacked by politics of power and debates that make the people – women and men – the key players in the ministry or mission. This is dangerous because it fails to recognise that first and foremost, ministry belongs to God. It is the Holy Spirit that calls, prepares and enables us for service in God's kingdom. Tensions and differences arise when one party or another think they know better who, what and how the calling to faithful discipleship should look like.

In his insightful commentary on the book of Acts, Prof Willie James Jennings notes that not Peter, nor Paul nor the early church are the main characters in Acts. Rather, Acts 'depicts life in the disrupting presence of the Spirit of God . . . [It] is the story of a God who desires us and all of creation and will not release us to isolations, social, economic, cultural, religious, gendered, and geographic.'[3] The ways God calls and forms disciples is not limited by the boundaries and divisions that mark human interactions. Furthermore, there is no one way the Spirit calls disciples; this diversity of how God works needs always to be kept in mind when we consider what it means to work in partnership in mission alongside other people whom God has also called. One of the beautiful results of how God calls disciples is precisely the multiplicity of gifts that each one brings. This is especially important to keep in mind when considering the ways in which women and men work together in ministry – each one brings her or his unique insights, talents and gifts. The shared mission would be that much weaker if it were carried out solo.

---

[3] Jennings, Willie James. *Acts*. Series *Belief: A Theological Commentary on the Bible*. Louisville: Westminster John Knox, 2017, pp. 1, 11.

Ministry goes beyond divisions

To consider seriously what partnership in mission looks like, we must pay careful attention to the boundaries and divisions that keep us apart and that hinder the growth of God's kingdom. There are numerous examples of this in the biblical texts. In Luke 5 we read one such example – the calling of the first disciples. There are lots of boundaries and power plays happening in this narrative: who needs healing and who does not; whose sins need forgiving and who gets to forgive . . . The things that kept the people together, the boundaries that defined their identities, such as the role of being a religious leader, are disrupted by the arrival of Jesus and his fishermen friends.

In Luke 5, Peter and his friends witness the healing of a leper and of a paralytic and then they are confronted with a huge challenge. After the affirmation, 'we have seen strange things today' (Luke 5:26), Jesus calls the next disciple, Levi, the tax-collector.

It is important to note that in that society, culture and religion, this joining together was not possible. Fishermen and tax-collectors belonged to two very different groups, two very different social levels. There was nothing normal, nothing natural about Peter and Levi (also known as 'Matthew' – see Matt 9:9) being put into the same group. Fishermen were at the bottom of the social scale; they were part of the family business and they tried to survive as people under the rule of a foreign power. Though probably poor and not highly educated, they were devout Jews, who tried to live faithfully – they went to prayers, followed the Mosaic laws and respected the words of the law keepers, the Pharisees. Fishermen were exploited by people like Levi. The tax-collector was the one who served the evil empire: the corrupt official who took money from his own people to give to the Romans and to pocket for himself. Levi was not just bad because he had money, but he was religiously an outsider, too.

What could Jesus be thinking? There was no way Peter and Levi could ever be friends. How could Jesus expect devout fishermen to go on a journey with a tax-collector? And yet, like Peter, we know Levi also accepted Jesus' invitation. So if Peter wanted to be near Jesus he would also have to be near Levi. Peter, who had given up his livelihood and even his name, his identity, to follow Jesus, was also quickly asked to welcome Levi into the newly formed group of other followers. Luke's narrative does not tell us what Peter's response was to the call to Levi and when a question is asked of the disciples about why they are eating with tax-collectors and sinners, it is Jesus who answers (Luke 5:30-31). Perhaps they had that sense of entitlement and resentment because the boundaries were being disturbed.

We do know of later struggles over money, over who was the greatest and other such disputes of power between the disciples.

Learning to be part of Jesus' kingdom, to be a disciple who cares for the vulnerable, the oppressed, the widow and the orphan, learning to be part of that kingdom meant for Peter (and for us!) learning to be with those whom he did not like. Even more than that – it meant learning a new kind of friendship and partnership for which Peter (and Levi) were completely unprepared. Both Peter and Levi were transformed by their calling and following Jesus. In a similar manner, men and women are transformed in and through a life of faithful discipleship. Often such transformation happens in the context of serving in mission together, just as it did for the fishermen and the tax-collector.

Being called to God's work and God's mission does not mean we are all called in the same manner nor does it make us all the same. It does mean we are together, as the narrative of Acts 2 and the coming of Pentecost indicate. God calls women and men to serve him in unity, not uniformity. God empowers and transforms them to be able to carry out God's mission.

One of the often overlooked portions of Paul's letters is the greetings he sends to the faithful at the end of a letter. Consider most of Romans 16 or the last 12 verses of 2 Timothy 4 . Though much has been made of Paul's writings about women in ministry and the divisions between men and women, perhaps it is time to consider more carefully these overlooked verses that are all about men and women serving together. Priscilla and Aquila, Mark, Trophimus, Claudia, Linus, Phoebe. The names go on and on. Paul asks his readers to greet them, to pray for them and insists that they are always in his prayers as well. Prayer is fundamental to overcome and transform divisions within the body of Christ and it is through this powerful tool that God's Spirit brings men and women together for partnership in God's kingdom.

Journey of discipleship

The journey of discipleship is one of getting closer to Jesus. As we get closer to Jesus we get closer to one another, and this is not always easy. In fact, it is often rather difficult because Jesus is the one choosing those who join the band. Like Peter, we would prefer to choose our own band mates, but that is not how God's Spirit does things.

Our Lord calls us to be one so that the world will know. By our love we are known, Jesus says in the gospel of John – this is a key part of that missionary calling of the people of God. Is the love Christians have towards one another the main sign that the world sees in us and in our partnerships? Boundaries are safer: they respect the power dynamics that give us our identity as church leaders and mission workers. Yet the disturbing lesson of the biblical texts is that if we want to be close to Jesus we will end up on a journey with people who look, feel and think differently than we do. If Christians are to be united by the Spirit and are to live in Christ, then we are going to have to be with others who are also called to be close to Jesus.

Peter and Levi had to learn to be brothers, to be together in community in a society, a culture, in economic and religious systems that told them over and over again: you are not friends, you should not be together. Their friendship, their sharing in ministry and learning to be disciples was only possible because of Jesus. Women and men are transformed not just by the calling upon their individual lives, but by the ways they learn to serve God's reign with one another and with all whom God calls.

Being close to Jesus, breaking down the boundaries of who is in and who is out is about inclusivity, but it is also about transformation – both Peter and Levi are changed. By being close to Jesus they are not made the same, but they are together. Who are we together with in mission and in life? Who is our neighbour? In Luke 10, Jesus' answer to the lawyer who asked him "Who is my neighbour?" is a story about those religious leaders who did not cross the boundary to help the wounded man, and the Samaritan who did.

The cultural drift is always towards rejecting anyone or any group that does not think, look or act like me – rejecting, othering, distancing, by claiming we do not belong to them. This is done by liberals and conservatives, this is done by humans. The alternative that Jesus offers is that mission is done together and that such partnerships break all the boundaries and systems within which we feel comfortable and know how to navigate.

Space in ministry

What we observe in the gospels is a pattern around Jesus' ministry. He is constantly creating a space around his own body where these conversations across divisions can take place and where genuine listening can emerge. Wherever he goes into ministry, to Galilee, to Samaria, home or away, even when he is invited to the more socially acceptable places, like the synagogue or the home of a Pharisee, Jesus is bringing other people with him who challenge those divisions and upset the paradigms of power and prejudice. Jesus changes the conversation and creates spaces for these difficult conversations around himself – the Syro-Phoenecian woman, the woman at the well, Jairus, the demoniac, Zacchaeus ... any narrative in which the transgression of the us/them occurs, where the "we know who is "us" and who is "them" is challenged. Jesus creates these spaces and tells his followers to love as he has loved.

If the church is the body of Christ, how are we creating these spaces for such challenges to the "us"/"them" paradigm? By being close to Jesus, people's religious and cultural expectations and their understanding of what is acceptable behaviour, are being challenged and turned upside down. Christian discipleship is a life of constantly learning anew and being open to the ways God transforms us and uses men and women together for the glory of God's kingdom.

What would it have felt like for Peter to be enmeshed, embedded because of his commitment to rabbi Jesus, to be together with a tax-collector like Levi? Why would that have been a difficult practice to live out? What would it have felt like to be a Christian leader in Jerusalem listening to Paul and Barnabas talk about the inclusion of those gentiles? That would have been every bit as scandalous to those Christian leaders in Jerusalem as a local congregation today trying to listen to discussions among the youth about sexuality, about politics or climate change. To be engaged in partnership for the sake of the gospel of Christ today means we cannot ignore these things.

Challenge for all Christians today

The challenge for Christians today to question boundaries and divisions is not for the sake of being progressive. Rather, it is recognising the pattern in Scripture that Jesus creates around himself – we cross boundaries because Jesus has already done so. It is about following Jesus and participating in the mission he has given us to do. Mission belongs to God and it is the Holy Spirit that does the calling. We should expect surprising and difficult partnerships on the road of discipleship. It is about learning to listen to God's Spirit speaking in and through people who surprise us.

Part of being the prophetic people of God means learning to discern and learning to expect God to surprise us. With confidence in God's character and love for God's people, the church is called to be that voice that preaches repentance and deliverance, even to our enemies. While we might be confident about our roles and our place, as was Peter, we are called to submit to the unusual things God is doing, giving up power and knowing that it is not up to us to solve everything, but that God will do things in God's time. We might not like God's time or ways. There is room for that discomfort, too, in partnership for God's mission. As we think about mission today, are we prepared to give up our desired outcomes, to withhold the power of judgement and submit to the fact that God will do things God's way, and that such ways might be very different than we anticipated or even prayed for? Partnership in God's mission will usually mean a 'laying down' of ourselves and our own agendas.

A fundamental question is: in our attempts to do mission together, to be sensitive towards other cultures and to learn about our differences, is Jesus still at the centre? Being partners in the gospel and doing mission together means telling the story of Jesus and discerning the gifts God has bestowed on everyone. Discipleship and partnership in mission are about spending time with God and listening to God, and then being faithful to God's call, being surprised and grateful for the unexpected people God calls to serve with us in the kingdom of Christ.

Reflection Questions

1. What experiences have you had working with people different from you? What have you learnt?

2. How have you made space for different people in the mission experiences that you have?

3. Who would be a modern equivalent to Peter and Levi in your context today? Or the woman at the well?

Overlooked Women in the Bible

Mary Evans

Introduction

This title could imply that we were going to consider whether, how and why the Bible overlooks women. However, that is not where this article is going as I am constantly surprised by how often the Bible speaks of and to women. What we are going to look at is how and why these references to women are overlooked when the Bible is read and taught, and what the implications are for our understanding. For example, one only needs to ask congregations about Huldah to note how few have heard of her; and even fewer realise that she was an important prophet used by God in Josiah's reformation and the first person in the Bible pictured as interpreting Scripture for others (2 Kings 22). From my perspective, one of the reasons for any overlooking is the fact that almost all theologians and biblical commentators have in the past been white, western, male and classically educated. The background of Greek philosophy has led to a largely unargued assumption that what we really need to concentrate on, particularly when looking at the Old Testament, is the doctrinal material found in the law and the prophets, with a secondary emphasis on poetic works and narratives.

The narratives of the historical books like Judges or Esther are often seen as secondary even though they make up a significant part of the biblical material. And it is in the narratives where we find the majority of references to particular women, so perhaps this has contributed to women being overlooked. The main significance of this narrative material is often seen as simply telling readers a story about what happened, and once it is clear that these events actually occurred, we can set them aside and use a very much edited approach to teach children's groups about the heroes of the Bible. This means that most of us are brought up (using UK film categories) with PG or U versions of the stories, when very many should be classified 15 or 18! When we do come to read the stories again, we skim over the details because we feel we already know the stories from our childhood.

Stories matter

But stories matter: especially in parts of the world where oral tradition is strong and especially for women who read and tell stories much more than men. More importantly, Bible narratives matter because they convey truths about God's character and action that we should not ignore.

In any case, in this article I am going to focus on stories, some briefly and one in more detail. The main purpose of this is to encourage readers to reread different biblical stories, concentrating on what the texts actually say rather than what we are expecting them to say.

Let me first recount some personal stories. A few weeks ago, I was watching a TV quiz show. The contestant did not know the story of David and Abigail came from the Bible. The 'expert's' comment on this was 'Yes, Abigail is one of the very few women mentioned in the Bible'. Why would she think that? Perhaps because, whether she attended church or not, she had only been introduced to a very few! Years ago, I was asked by a publisher to review a projected book providing an easy overview of the Old Testament. It was well written and helpful. But in this overview, there were only two sentences (yes, just two sentences!) mentioning women, one referred to Eve and one to Deborah. I am fairly certain this did not indicate that the author had a negative view of women, but rather stemmed from his conclusion that limited space meant concentrating on 'important' things. For him that meant doctrinal teaching, national leaders and international conflicts.

Last year I was asked to give a series of talks on Judges to a mixed audience of people from bible focussed churches. One older lady who converted to Christianity about five years ago and had attended church regularly since then, came up afterwards to tell me how excited she had been a few weeks previously to read about Deborah in the Bible. She had never heard of her before! It is an interesting fact that many Bible Dictionaries have an article entitled 'Women'. When asked to write one of these I enquired who was going to write the one on 'Men' so we could compare notes. But of course, no such article existed. The editors, wonderful Christian men, had never considered that this created an impression that women are peripheral in the Old Testament, that it is really about and for men, with women being a side-topic needing to be considered separately. In trying to recognise women, they were perhaps only compounding the problem.

Stories in Scripture

So, let us consider some examples of stories in Scripture where a different perspective might bring new insight – for ALL readers, (another common misconception is that all stories are relevant to women, but the stories relating to women are not particularly relevant to men and can be 'relegated' to be looked at in women's conferences) Firstly, Judges 13 where a woman who is unnamed, (probably deliberately given the way the story develops), takes centre stage. She and her husband Manoah are portrayed throughout the Samson narratives as a couple who have a good relationship and, in a time noted for evil and unfaithfulness to God, seem to be seeking to serve Him. This woman was childless, unable to give birth – the tautology emphasises how significant this tragedy was in her life. 'The angel of the Lord appeared to the woman when she was alone, and his first words were 'You are barren'! One might at first glance think this was a cruel approach, but it can also be read as showing that God was only too aware that this was on her mind all the time. The fantastically welcome message is that she is going to have a son – and instructions are given as to how the boy is to be brought up, how she too is to behave, and that he 'will begin to deliver Israel'. That somewhat ambiguous phrase clearly deserves a lot of unpacking but that is not for this article.

The woman's first thought was to find Manoah and tell him. It is perhaps significant that she speaks first of the visitor and her sense of awe and the reluctance she felt to question him. Only then does she tell of the promise given, despite its life changing importance. Manoah's first thought was to pray that the visitor would come again, presumably so he too could hear the message. The next verse has ironic, even comic overtones: God heard Manoah's prayer and answered it by coming back to the woman when she was on her own 'out in the field', presumably working; the partnership between the couple in managing their property is perhaps evidenced here. (The Old Testament refers several times to women in employment, including Boaz's female workers whom Ruth joined, and the ideal woman of Proverbs 31. In fact, there are more references to women working than there are examples of women pictured in the home looking after the children, often described as 'traditional' or the 'Biblical ideal'. That is not to say that is not how it was, but it is harder than might be expected to argue for that view from the Old Testament.)

The woman ran to tell her husband who 'followed' her back. He then asks how the promised boy is to be brought up, but that question is not answered, the angel only speaks of how the wife herself is to behave. Anything else he wants to know, he must learn from her.

When I first studied this chapter, every commentary I could find at that time saw the passage as illustrating the belief that a woman's testimony was less valuable than that of a man. But only one, which happened to be written by a woman, noted that the writer clearly brings out the fact that God himself did not share that view. As the story draws to a close, we see more evidence that the woman grasped truths more easily than her husband. She had realised this visitor was special and it was inappropriate to question him: Manoah does probe the stranger and is told his question is not appropriate. He wants to honour the visitor and is told to honour the Lord. When he finally accepts that their visitor was the angel of the Lord, he is petrified they will die, whereas his pragmatic wife is sure that God would not have promised them a son if they were both to die now! It is hard to see how one can read this passage without seeing the deliberate way in which the woman's role is emphasised, and to be fair, most modern commentators do pick up on the centrality of the woman in this passage. But for many generations, this was not even noticed and even today this passage is not one to which most Christians have had their attention drawn.

Have you noticed?

There are several other narratives where the writers show very clearly that they understand the culture surrounding them but also write about it in a way that critiques that culture. One of these 'have you noticed' stories is that of Hagar. She was a foreign, female slave and probably in line with that status, neither Abraham nor Sarah ever address or refer to her by name. She is 'my servant', 'your servant', or 'that slave woman'. In that society she, and her wishes, were of no account. But God didn't share that view. When Hagar runs away to the desert and encounters God, the first thing the angel of the Lord does is address her by name! She may not have been the mother of the promised son, but God recognised her as a person who mattered. Another often un-noticed point here is that although Isaac is usually spoken of as 'the son of Abraham', Genesis 17 makes it very clear that he was also to be the son of Sarah. Abraham would have been quite happy for Ishmael to have counted (Genesis 17:18), but it is made explicit that both the father and the mother of the promised child were chosen by God.

Also 'have you noticed' the way in which the writer in 2 Samuel 13 picks up on the terrible distress of Tamar when her brother abuses and then expels her, by describing the change in clothing from the 'richly ornamented robe' of a princess to the torn clothing and ashes of the unloved outsider. Her feelings mattered nothing to her brother and little to her father, but the text makes it clear that they did matter to the writer and to God.

The last chapters of Judges tell another story of the terrible mistreatment of women: the Levite's partner and then the young women of Jabesh Gilead. The writer manages to tell these stories in a way that makes clear the cavalier attitude to women in that society but also causes the reader to feel anger about their treatment. I am convinced that that was done very skilfully and very deliberately to highlight the cruel plight of the women.

There are also negative 'have you noticed' things concerning women which we can learn from. None of the women of Bethlehem who with the whole town were 'stirred', when Naomi and Ruth arrived there, did anything to help and support them until after Ruth had married an important rich man. And Esther, usually portrayed entirely as a heroine, succumbs to the violence of her age: when she had found a way to change the king's ruling that all Jews should be killed, she joined in the genocide of others without evidence of their actual guilt – and when asked by the king if she would like anything else, the only thing she can think of is for another day of terrible revenge, outstripping Haman's cruelty.

All of this is intended to encourage a further in-depth reading of narratives looking beyond the surface to the significantly added details. And for us to do that we must learn to ask other people's questions, not just those formulated by western, classically educated males. We need to ask questions from the perspective of people like Samaritans, or poor widows or a lame beggar so that our perspective is shifted. In today's context, this must involve asking women's questions, and those coming from Africans, Asians, Latin Americans and all those in God's world who have a different perspective from us. As the old hymn says, 'The Lord has yet more light and truth to bring forth from his word'. Let's look out for it!

Reflection Questions

1. It does seem as if men and women ask different questions and notice different things when they read the biblical stories. How important do you think it is that we listen to and learn from each other in order to get a fuller picture of what the text might be teaching us?

2. Are there other stories where, perhaps due to your own circumstances, you have noticed something in the text that has not been raised when the stories have been told to you? Discuss with others whether what you noticed was something that the text really does suggest, but readers with a different background might have missed.

Women Participating as Equal Partners in the Mission of God

Peirong Lin

Introduction

Stories shapes our lives. When I was young, I grew up with an eclectic mix of stories. This ranged from Disney princesses to eastern mythologies like the Journey to the West. These stories have influenced me subtly and have shaped my preferences—what I believed was worth pursuing, what I believed was appropriate for a woman, what I "wanted to be when I grew up". At times, they have also unnecessarily burdened me with expectations of what it means to be a woman. In these stories, princesses were often portrayed as damsels in distress, awaiting rescue by a prince in shining armour. Alternatively, in eastern mythologies, women were portrayed either as merciful and sacrificial, or vixen-like *femmes fatales* who can cause the death of holy people like the beloved monk.

As Christians, the main story that should influence us is the story of God's mission as described in the Bible. This narrative is typically summarized as the God of purpose who created the world, fall caused by human rebellion, God's redemptive plan and the future hope of new creation.[4] As God's people, we are to participate in this mission of God for the redemption of the whole creation.

A woman's story is both unique and common to humankind. Some female experiences are distinctive: biological experiences such as childbirth, violence against women, the trafficking of women for sexual purposes. At the same time, created in the image of God, both women and men share in a common humanity. God called the creation of humankind good and gave them a common command.

This chapter traces the narrative of the mission of God through the perspective of a woman. It argues that the manner of participation of humankind – in partnership – is rooted in the creation story. Together, men and women share in the future hope of new creation.

---

[4] One helpful resource that further expounds on this concept is Christopher J. H. Wright, *The Mission of God: Unlocking the Bible's Grand Narrative* (Nottingham: Inter-Varsity Press, 2006).

Women and men – created in partnership

> ²⁶ Then God said, "Let us make man in our image, after our likeness. And let them have dominion over the fish of the sea and over the birds of the heavens and over the livestock and over all the earth and over every creeping thing that creeps on the earth."
>
> ²⁷ So God created man in his own image,
> in the image of God he created him;
> male and female he created them.
>
> ²⁸ And God blessed them. And God said to them, "Be fruitful and multiply and fill the earth and subdue it and have dominion over the fish of the sea and over the birds of the heavens and over every living thing that moves on the earth." ²⁹ And God said, "Behold, I have given you every plant yielding seed that is on the face of all the earth, and every tree with seed in its fruit. You shall have them for food.
> (Gen 1:26-28)

God created both men and women as special representatives of God. Individually, they are described as image bearers of God. As such, they enjoy special standing in creation, differentiated from other creatures. They are exceptionally chosen to be recipients of God's love and are more esteemed within his creation (Matt 6:26). Made in God's image, they are also the recipient of God's commands to be fruitful, multiply, fill and subdue the earth, and have dominion. Both men and women are meant to be representatives of God in the way they deal with the rest of creation, reflecting the nature of God to creation.[5]

Being in the image of God "describes human life in relationship with God and with other creatures. ... To be human is to live freely and gladly in relationships of mutual respect and love ... It expresses self-transcending life in relationship with others – with the 'wholly other' we call God, and with all those different 'others' who need our help and whose help we also need in order to be the human creatures God intends us to be."[6]

Found in the core of God's blessings, true partnership between men and women is intended in the creation story. This involves men and women working together in every area of life to represent God in creation.

---

[5] Stanley J. Grenz, *Theology for the Community of God* (Carlisle: Paternoster Press, 1994), 230.

[6] Daniel L. Migliore, *Faith Seeking Understanding: An Introduction to Christian Theology* (Grand Rapids: Eerdmans Publishing, 2004), 145.

Humans are not made to work in isolation but in relationship. As they are created in the image of the triune God, this relationship should be marked by mutual love and service modelled after the different persons in the Trinity. "The persons of the Trinity speak with each other, plan with each other, obey each other, act for each other, care for each other, honour each other, etc., and all these actions are related to love."[7]

Created lower than Adam?

God did not reserve blessings for one sex from the other. There was no mention of a particular hierarchical order between men and women. Eve was created as an indispensable help for Adam and the whole of humankind to reach God's commands together. In Genesis 2:20b-23, Eve was created to provide companionship to Adam as well as to be a help. This understanding of help is exceptional and valuable, something that the rest of creation cannot provide. So valuable was this help that the same term *'ezer*, used to describe what Eve was to Adam, is also used to describe God's help to humankind in times of urgent need (Ps 33:20; Ps 70:5; Ps 115:9). In partnership, Adam and Eve work together as God's representatives.

Fall

As we all know, the story of humankind did not stay in the perfect state of creation. The fall is an undeniable aspect of the human condition. One reason why both Eve and Adam chose to disobey God's commands was their desire to be like God. In this regard, sin has been described as "resistance to our essential relation to God and our need of God's grace."[8] A relational understanding of sin goes beyond the understanding of sin as disobedience or the violation of a moral code.

Sin results in failure, "our inability to fulfill God's design for us."[9] We fail and fall short of God's glory (Romans 3:23). As a result, we are unable to reflect what God is truly like to creation. Generally, the ways in which men and women fail differ. Whereas men fail and miss the mark through "a wilful, prideful manner, many women have discovered that they are more likely to fail God's ideal by too readily acquiescing to the domination

---

[7] Thomas Schirrmacher, *Missio Dei: God's Missional Nature* (Bonn: Verlag für Kultur und Wissenschaft, 2017), 53.
[8] Daniel L. Migliore, *Faith Seeking Understanding*, 155.
[9] Stanley J. Grenz, *Theology for the Community of God*, 241.

of others. In their self-abnegation, women readily assume that the curse of Genesis 3 is their place in creation rather than a distortion of it."[10]

One big consequence of the fall is the distortion of the original understanding of partnership between men and women. The fall changed the relationships that men and women would have. Whereas God's blessings and commands described earlier were intended for both men and women, the consequences are particular to each gender. For the women, these consequences include "pains in childbearing, desire for one's husband and the husband ruling over her" (Gen 3:16). These consequences complicate the relationship, changing an equal relationship to one that is subjugated to the rule of men. The desire a woman has for her husband is now easily exploitable. Finally, the curse also taints the experience of having children.

Woman entangled in the consequences of the fall

The lives of Sarah and Naomi are described as examples of women living in the consequences of the fall.

Sarah

Sarah's movements were determined by the men in her life.[11] She travelled with her husband Abraham, her father Terah, and her nephew from Ur to Haran and settled there (Gen 11:31). Years later, she moved again with Abraham from Haran and set out for the land of Canaan following Abraham's call from God (Gen 12:4). After reaching Canaan, the land that her husband believed was given to them by God, they had to move again to Egypt because of a famine (Gen 12:10). Decisions about where they were living were not hers to make.

Sarah's love for Abraham was used against her. When they reached Egypt, Abraham asked her not to disclose the fact that he was her husband (Gen 12:13). Arguing that her beauty might cause his death since he was her husband, he told her to call him her brother. Although Abraham was indeed her half-brother, he was very much her husband too (Gen 20:12). This was not a one-time event either, but a pattern of behaviour. A similar account was recorded in Gerar, where Abimelech, King of Gerar sent for Sarah and took her (Gen 20). Abraham again acted in his own interest, to

---

[10] Stanley J. Grenz, *Theology for the Community of God*, 242.
[11] To avoid unnecessary confusion, I use the names Sarah and Abraham throughout, even though both had different names at the beginning of the story.

save his own life. He appealed to her love for him in making his requests (Gen 20:13). He was not concerned about the possibility of her being given sexually to another. Sarah was indeed harmed by this self-centred act of Abraham in Egypt. She was taken to the palace and Abraham was given animals and servants (Gen 12:15–16). God had to intervene in both situations to ultimately save Sarah (Gen 12:17, 20:3).

Much of the account of Sarah in the Old Testament was related to her desire for children. These pains started long before the physical act of birth and caused Sarah to inflict pain on others. In the first descriptions of Sarah, she is introduced as Abraham's wife who was unable to conceive (Gen 11:30). Despite the promise given to her husband that he would have descendants (Gen 12:15), she gave up hope and came up with her own solution. She asked Abraham to sleep with her maidservant, Hagar, so that "perhaps I can build a family through her" (Gen 16:2). This painful obsession to have her own child led her to neglect the humanity of her maidservant Hagar. The pain endured by Sarah was spread to another. When Hagar became pregnant, the relationship between Sarah and Hagar continued to disintegrate. Hagar despised Sarah (Gen 16:4), leading Sarah to mistreat her (Gen 16:6).

After what seemed like a lifetime of disappointment, Sarah finally gave birth to Isaac. But this was not the end of her troubles related to children. The child whom Hagar bore, Ishmael, never became the "family" that Sarah thought he could be. Ishmael was caught mocking Isaac during the feast given for him (Gen 21:9). Finally, she would again be ruthless in asking Abraham to "get rid" of Hagar and Ishmael as she did not want them to have any share of Isaac's inheritance (Gen 21:10).

Naomi

Naomi is introduced in the book of Ruth at the height of her misery. She was about to move back to her homeland after experiencing profound loss as a migrant in Moab. She and her family had relocated to Moab to escape the famine in Bethlehem (Ruth 1:2). While there, her husband died leaving her with her two sons (Ruth 1:3). These two sons married Moabites and, after about ten years, died too (Ruth 1:4-5).

Naomi's existence was very much determined by the men in her life. She was the wife of Elimelech and the mother of Mahlon and Kilion. When the men died, she felt that she had nothing left. This compelled her to ask her daughters-in-law to leave, since she had nothing left to offer them (Ruth 1:11). The men also mediated her relationship with God. Naomi's husband was the one who decided that they should move to Moab from

Bethlehem (Ruth 1:1). During that time, moving to a different land was akin to leaving the protection of their God. Therefore, in effect Elimelech took things into his own hands during the famine by moving the family to Moab. When he died, the sons married foreign wives, putting down further roots in Moab. When these two men also died, Naomi blamed God despite the fact that it was the men who made the decisions to relocate to Moab and settle there.

The subsequent redemption of Naomi in the story of Ruth also illustrates the patriarchal system that these women had to navigate. When they returned to Bethlehem, they had to find a way to survive by themselves. Ruth gleaned in the field and picked up leftover grain (Ruth 2:2). She was in an unsafe situation and at the mercy of the owner of the field (Ruth 2:22). She attained safety only because she found favour with the field's owner, Boaz (Ruth 2:8-9). To ensure security and a home for Ruth, Naomi played matchmaker between Ruth and Boaz (Ruth 3:1). She taught Ruth how to indicate interest by lying at Boaz's feet (Ruth 3:4), kickstarting the process that led Boaz to become their kinsman redeemer (Ruth 4:1-10). Ruth and Boaz eventually married and had a son, Obed. This boy that gave her and Naomi standing in society. Obed's existence meant that Naomi now had an heir.

The stories of Sarah and Naomi are not unique. As in other stories of women recorded in the Old Testament, the suffering they experience can be linked to the fall. Even today, these consequences remain. Women continue to be surrounded by patriarchy, sex trafficking, infertility and other forms of family issues. This deep brokenness cannot be remedied by humankind alone. God, through his son Jesus, came and provided a way for redemption. Brokenness does not need to define women's existence. His reign, the kingdom of God, can bring light into these difficult situations.

Redemption

Jesus came to this earth as the Messiah. He provided a way for humankind to be reconciled back to God. In his ministry, Jesus often preached that the kingdom of God was at hand (Mk 1:15). This kingdom of God is not a place on earth. It is the person of Jesus (Luke 17:21). He represents the reign of God on earth, the reality of the kingdom in human form.

Through his life, death and resurrection, the world is reconciled to Jesus, the son of God. This reconciliation involves more than personal salvation. As John Stott wrote, "The kingdom of God is God's dynamic rule, breaking into human history through Jesus, confronting, combating and overcoming evil, spreading the wholeness of personal and communal well-being, taking possession of his people in total blessing and total demand."[12] God's purpose for this earth is for all and not the select few. What is done on earth matters to God. In the Lord's Prayer, we pray for the kingdom of God to come on earth, not just in heaven.

This kingdom of God invites an active response from all, a partnership of men and women working together in every area of life. "The harvest is plentiful, but the workers are few" (Lk 10:2). There is much to do to break the darkness in different areas of life. Responding to the message of God's reign involves being a faithful witness of Christ, revealing the kingdom of God during this period of Jesus' ascension and his return.[13] This includes reflecting on one's life story based on the larger narrative of God's, modelling one's mission on Christ's mission.[14] Jesus intentionally entered the brokenness of this world so that he was able to identify with people in their actual situations.[15] In the same way, our personal mission in this world should include deliberate solidarity with the broken world, including the plight of women today.

We respond to the brokenness in this world as his image bearers, recognising Christ as the ultimate image of God.[16] As the Son of Man, he is our example of the perfect image bearer. As part of humankind, we have the potential to live out God's commands, but we will never be able to reach that potential by themselves. We can truly function as image bearers "insofar as the Spirit works Christlikeness" in us.[17] In line with the theme of this book, the question then is, what are some specifics that women, myself included, can learn from Jesus as the image bearer?

Women participating as part of the body of Christ

Women have a unique place in the body of Christ. Their lives and unique experiences matter. We should unabashedly participate in this kingdom of God in all areas of our lives. This participation is done in a spirit of collaboration. Together, men and women form the body of Christ. As the triune God exists in community, we, made in this image, are also communal in nature.

---

[12] John Stott, *Issues Facing Christians Today* (Grand Rapids: Zondervan, 2006), 56.
[13] Leslie Newbigin, *The Gospel in a Pluralist Society* (London: SPCK, 1989), 125.
[14] John Stott, *Issues Facing Christians Today*, 55.
[15] Ibid., 55.
[16] Stanley J. Grenz, *Theology for the Community of God*, 224.
[17] Ibid.

Being part of the body of Christ recognizes that we are responsible for each other. "We are created for life in community with others, to exist in relationships of mutual fidelity and mutual freedom in fellowship."[18] "If one part suffers, every part suffers with it; if one part is honoured, every part rejoices with it" (1 Cor 12:26). The first step of being responsible for the other involves taking seriously the different living conditions of all members of the body of Christ.

Service as power

Taking seriously the living conditions involves being mindful of the existing power structures within the Christian community and in the world. Power exists in all relationships. Although the presence of power in itself is not negative, it has been abused for self-serving reasons at the expense of the other. In Philippians 2:1-8, we are reminded of how Christ, who is all powerful, made himself weak and vulnerable for the sake of saving humankind. He did not use his equality with God for self-serving reasons. He focused on others and gave all he could for them. In the same way, we can use whatever power we have in the service of the other. We can shine light on areas of oppression. Power is used to engage in the struggle of making the world into God's home.[19]

Identification with the other

Women can also use their circumstances as a catalyst for change. Often, women can feel like the "other", discriminated against because of their sex. They experience the power inequality in various settings. While this inequity is certainly not ideal, this state of brokenness can also direct one's attention to God. Jesus said, "Blessed are the poor in spirit, for theirs is the kingdom of heaven." (Matt 5:3). Difficult situations can prod us to become willing to move out of the status quo.

Jesus did not operate within existing manmade limitations. During his ministry, he "transgressed the supposed boundaries of God's grace and thus shocked the sensibilities of the guardians of religious tradition."[20] He disturbed the status quo of his time and went against social norms. In the

---

[18] Daniel L. Migliore, *Faith Seeking Understanding*, 149.
[19] Miroslav Volf & Matthew Croasmun, *For the life of the World: Theology that makes a difference* (Grand Rapids: Brazos Press, 2019),51.
[20] Migliore, *Faith Seeking Understanding*, 180.

same way, a woman can develop solidarity with those who are oppressed and work towards bringing justice and God's rule into the situation.

Future hope

We live in the tension of the now and not yet. Challenges continue even as a Christian. In participating in this mission of God, we can rest in the hope of the promise of God's second coming, and of a new heaven and new earth. The struggles and suffering experienced today pales in comparison to what we can hope for.

The late missionary, author and public speaker Elisabeth Elliot was no stranger to suffering. While being missionaries, her first husband, Jim Elliot was murdered by the people with whom they were trying to share the gospel. Her second husband, a theological professor died of cancer four years after their marriage. Such experiences did not leave her embittered. In her suffering, she remembered that God remained her refuge. The Christian God was faithful and there was something amazing to look forward to at life's end. She described the joy set before us, the comfort she found in Romans 8:18. "Suffering is nothing compared to the coming glory that is going to be revealed to us." What is experienced is temporal and pales in comparison to the promised glory of God.[21]

In this new reality, sin will be no more and we will be filled with God's glory and holiness. God promises His blessings in this new heaven and earth, where all tears will be wiped away. There will be full fellowship with Christ with full knowledge and eternal rest. This is promised to all of God's people, men and women. It is the promised end in the Bible's grand narrative. This is truly worth hoping for.

May we not shy away from discomfort or suffering. Rather, may the mission of God centre our lives and orient us as we in partnership participate in this mission of God!

Reflection Questions:

1. What stories have influenced you in becoming the woman you are today? How does the mission of God inform your life?

2. Based on your current life situation, how can you actively participate in the mission of God?

---

[21] For more details, see her book Elisabeth Elliot, *A Path through Suffering*, (Grand Rapids: Revell, 2021).

Galatians 3:28: a Vision for Partnership

Samuel Oluwatosin Okanlawon

Introduction

Previous studies on the Christian perspective on gender equality, with or without exegetical analyses of Galatians 3:28 (Uchem 2005; Kohm 2008; Aune 2010; Casmir et al 2014; Lusey et al 2017; Vorster 2019; Wood 2019), have not linked it to the concept of women suffering persecution. What biblical template can we follow to enable women and girls to express their spiritual giftedness and being in our ecclesial communities without any restrictions? How do we incorporate women into the holistic ministry of the church and enable them to participate fully in society?

Two Pauline texts used to restrict women's participation in the church are indicative of Christian gender inequality: 1 Corinthians 11:2–16 and 1 Timothy 2:11–15. Debated passages such as these should be interpreted in the light of clearer ones like Galatians 3:28. The roles assigned to women have been largely influenced by cultural, religious, and economic factors rather than by their capacities as the creation of God and as part of God's redeemed. This has resulted in women being confined to domestic chores, and to the bearing and rearing of children (Kasomo 2010:129), which has led to widespread acceptance of the unbiblical norm that to be a woman is to be neglected. Unequal power relationships and structures within the Church and society create room for gender inequality/inequity and the persecution of women.

Gender inequality is defined as culturally and socially created differences between men and women that cause the two sexes not to have the same share in decision-making and wealth production (Wood 2019). Equality does not mean that women and men become the same but that women's and men's opportunities and responsibilities do not depend on whether they are born male or female (Bird & Carroll 2016).

On the other hand, persecution generally involves the unfair treatment and subjugation of an individual or group by another individual or group and the cumulative effect of numerous harms that affect a person's subjective psychological make-up (Kelly 1993:645). Given the focus of this paper, the definition of persecution proposed here as it relates to the persecution of women, is the stereotyping practices that hold women back from their full potential and from participating fully and equally in all spheres of life. This ranks as one of the worst forms of violence against women.[22]

This paper examines the Pauline paradigm, "There is neither male nor female," in Galatians 3:28 as a faith-based approach to counter practices that prevent women and girls from fully expressing their God-given capabilities and personhood within the Christian community and society. The aim is to promote gender equity and affirmation of females rather than simply to push for gender equality. This serves as a template to reinterpret those misinterpreted biblical passages used to subjugate women in the church and as a tool of oppression. The relevant data come from analysis of the biblical texts, along with published materials on patriarchy, gender (in)equality and the persecution of women. I draw on J. G. Vander Watt's hermeneutic theory of contextual relevance, which emphasizes the links we draw between the world of the biblical text and that of the interpreter.

Patriarchy and the persecution of women and the attendant challenges

In Van Huffel's words, "Patriarchy is a social system that promotes hierarchies and awards economic, political and social power to one group over others. Patriarchy is essentially androcentric and hierarchical by nature" (2011:259). Cockburn, as cited by Dogo (2014:263), describes patriarchy as a system in which leadership, authority, aggressiveness and responsibility reside in men and masculinity, while nurture, compliance, passivity and dependence are the part of women and femininity. Ideologically, patriarchy upholds the view that the male has control over women and all others under their care (Wood 2019). Theologically, patriarchy has deeply shaped our perceptions of God and the subsequent relations with humanity. As such, "The voice of God is the voice of man" (Ackermann 1992:25). Women and girls become highly disadvantaged.

Patriarchal systems of the church and society have entrenched cultural stereotypes that elevate male-dominated structures, strengthen the masculine-feminine dichotomy, and subsequently discriminate against women and minimize the roles they play. This has caused women to internalize a sense of inferiority to men. As Van Huffel (2011:264–65) hints, legislation, ratification of international and regional instruments and formulation of numerous gender policies are insufficient to promote gender equality/equity because the root causes of gender injustices lie in the

---

[22] In this paper, the word "women" is used to comprise all females, women and girls.

patriarchal structures of the society. Therefore, only the unbundling and deconstruction of the intrinsic patriarchal structures of our society can engender gender equality/equity.

According to Freedman (2015:45), women worldwide are subject to a wide range of violent and persecutory treatments which are related to their social, economic and political status as women. The persecution of women can be through traditional practices such as female genital mutilation, forced marriage or dowry; forced abortion or sterilization; rape; or domestic violence/intimate partner violence (IPV). Most often, the varied forms of persecution of women either go unnoticed and unpunished, or are spoken of in hushed tones. Women may be persecuted by family members, acquaintances, neighbours, or men in positions of power and authority. And the persecution could be cross-cultural, cross-national, interreligious, or intra-religious.

In the context of the church, persecution has been predicated on a people's or institutional distaste for Christians or Christianity (Mahendra 2016:33). Hence, persecution is seen as coming from outside the church rather than from within. Many persecutory acts against women and girls that bar or limit them from expressing their capabilities are often not categorized as "persecution" because they are not physical.

Some of the resultant effects of the patriarchy and persecution of women in the larger society include, but are not limited to, the following: transnational migration, poor physical and mental health, demoralization, stigmatization, low self-esteem, inferiority complex, prevention of the full advancement of women, robbing women of their divine identity, and neglect.

The church is not exempted from expressions of gender injustice and inequality. This is experienced as constructs of power and privilege within the cultural patriarchy of power mongers (Casimir *et al* 2014:172). In the early church as recorded in the Bible, women were recognized and appreciated as they participated in the church as deacons, as companions of Paul and other apostles, and even as apostles or church leaders themselves (Romans 16:3–7); moreover, they performed pastoral functions that included teaching, catechizing to other women and caring for the sick (Kasomo 2010:130). This valuation of women was however not followed through by the early church fathers. They used texts from the Bible (Genesis 1:27; 2:20–23; 3:1–24; 1 Corinthians 11:7–9; 14:33–35; Ephesians 5:22–23; 1 Timothy 2:8–15) to legitimate the marginalisation and subordination and oppression of women (Wood 2019). This has caused women's status to become vilified and diminished.

Text of Galatians 3:28

οὐκ ἔνι Ἰουδαῖος οὐδὲ Ἕλλην, οὐκ ἔνι δοῦλος οὐδὲ ἐλεύθερος, οὐκ ἔνι ἄρσεν καὶ θῆλυ· πάντες γὰρ ὑμεῖς εἷς ἐστε ἐν Χριστῷ Ἰησοῦ.

There is neither Jew nor Gentile, neither slave nor free, nor is there male and female, for you are all one in Christ Jesus (NIV).

To understand what Paul means in Galatians 3:28, we must determine the overall message of the book of Galatians by establishing the historical and literary context and by considering the central idea or thesis statement of the verse (Martin 1979:226–227).

The social context of Galatia when Paul wrote was that Greeks divided all persons into two classes, Greeks and barbarians, whereas the Jews called all other persons "goyim" (Stamm 1981:519). Distinctions between people were taken very seriously. Two dominant themes have been identified as Paul's motifs in the Epistle to the Galatians: the justification of the believer in the Lord Jesus Christ apart from legal works, and the ministry of the Holy Spirit as the indwelling energizer of the spiritual life in Christ (Johnson 2005). The Judaizing heresy, whereby Jewish Christians were compelling the Gentile Christians to live by Jewish practices (1:6–7; 5:2–3.12; 6:11–15), and circumcision in particular, had become prevalent in Galatia (Donovan 2016).

The Judaizers were demanding Torah observance. When Paul wrote this letter, there was a deep division between Jews and Gentiles within the body of Christ. The Mediterranean world at that time was a male-dominated hierarchical society where people were perceived and treated according to the social standards of superiority and inferiority (Aune 2010:176). Thus, the immediate context of Galatians 3:28 is Paul's exposition of the law, that is, to be a slave-guardian on the path toward maturity and unrestricted enjoyment of sonship (cf. 3:24; 4:1–7). Sonship in Christ has resulted in freedom that has released all categories of persons from bondage to the Old Covenant to negate the claims of the Judaizers in Galatia.

Galatians 3:28 is part of a paragraph that commences at vv. 26–27: "For you are all sons of God through faith in Jesus Christ. For as many of you as were baptized into Christ have put on Christ" (NKJV). This is Paul's affirmation of the believers' status in Christ. He then mentions, in v. 28, a triple pair of distinctions, by ethnicity, social class and gender. The verse emphasizes the vertical consequence of salvation for the believer (i.e. our relationship to God). "There is no male or female" is followed by "You are all one in Christ Jesus."

Structurally, Grobler (2011) notes that Galatians 3:28 is composed of three negated couplets as well as an explanatory clause. Two of these couplets are positioned within the recipe that "there is neither" X ουδε Y (X nor Y), but the third couplet, which is our main focus, contains a slight variation: "there is neither male "καὶ" (and) female." A different combination is apparently used here to connect two contrasting nouns. Degner (2001) says that the reason is not totally clear, but that when "male" (ἔνι ἄρσεν) occurs with "female" (θῆλυ), the couplet is almost always καὶ. Hove (1999:67-68) argues that the variation, in conjunction with the third pair, is an intentional reference to Genesis, where God created humanity as "male and female" prior to the Fall, and it was very good (Genesis 1:27.31).

The three pairs of phrases in the text, as noted above, point to the varied implications of Paul's corporate Christology (salvation in Christ): neither Jew nor Gentile, addressing ethnic distinctions, and neither "slave nor free", addressing social status distinctions. Tolmie (2014:108-109) states that most published works on the text indicate that the third pair, "neither male nor female", hints that gender differences do not matter anymore as a result of our connection to Christ. This does not imply that gender differences have been abolished, but that being male or female does not bring any disadvantage. Witherington opines that the rhetorical function of Paul's assertion in the verse might have been to counter the opponents' attempt to re-establish the patriarchal order of things in the Galatian church (2009:113-120). Paul replaces the importance attached to physical maleness with an ethics of mutuality.

Notably, Heidebrecht (2005:187) states that Paul uses a different Greek conjunction with the male/female couplet that is not used with the other couplets, although not all Bible translations reflect this difference. The use of "and" instead of "or" more probably reflects the wording of Genesis 1:27: "So God created humankind in his image, in the image of God he created them; male and female" (NRSV). Paul expresses a negation of the distinction expressed in the original sexual differentiation of humanity. The explanatory clause "you are all one in Christ" gives the reason for the abrogation of the distinctions mentioned earlier. Paul's assertion that all Christians are "one person" (εις, masculine) in Christ does not mean that they lose their individuality (Stamm 1981:520). It implies that every Christian is to reflect the Christ-life, each from his own angle of social and human constitution. The oneness of the Christians with Christ and with each other was organic and vital. There is diversity in unity as well as unity in diversity (cf. 1 Corinthians 12-14).

On the other hand, the expression in verse 28 relates to Paul's assertions in the preceding verse 27, which likewise restates the truth of verse 26. In verse 27, Paul says that the baptized have "put on Christ". To put on Christ as a garment, in the context of the Epistle to the Galatians, means that the person is justified (cf. Isaiah 61:10). So Paul reinforces the truth that God regards all persons who are baptized—that is, those who have become Christians—as "sons", regardless of their status or societal distinctions. Those who are included in the *pantes* (for all) of verse 26 and the *huioi* (sons) of verse 26 are not diverse and divided. They are no longer under the Law but are *heis*, one person in Christ.

Interpreting Galatians 3:28 in relation to patriarchy and the persecution of women

Paul's view of women's roles changes from one biblical/ecclesial context to another. He urges seemingly women to be subordinate to men in the Corinthian church on the basis of Genesis chapter 2 (1 Corinthians 11:7-9); he demands women to keep silent in the churches in accordance to the law and not to exert authority over a man (1 Corinthians 14:34; 1 Timothy 2:12). Kasomo (2010:132) asserts that this is one of the many evidences of Paul's rabbinical conflict and Christian insight. We must keep in mind that those biblical texts that are considered derogatory to women reflect the exigencies of culture and tradition of the times and the particular context of both the biblical authors and interpreters.

Paul's declaration that there is "neither male and female" stands in marked contrast to commonly accepted patterns of privilege and prejudice in the ancient world. Women were considered inferior within both Jewish and Greek culture. Hellenistic men regularly thanked God for allowing them to be born as human beings and not as beasts, as Greeks and not as barbarians, as citizens and not as slaves—and as men and not as women. Jewish men commonly recited a prayer each morning which stated, "I thank thee, God, that thou hast not made me a slave or a woman or a Gentile dog" (Esler 2014).

Hence, Paul is emphasizing in Galatians 3:26-28 that men and women enjoy a new, equal and exalted status before God. Thus, the female gender has been raised from degradation and denigration. Earthly relationships are put in the perspective of salvation history. All persons in Christ have the same salvation status before God, though they do not necessarily have the same function. There are no ethnic, economic or gender distinctions. This was contrary to the cosmopolitanism promoted by Paul's contemporaries (i.e. Greek philosophers) in the first century. Paul promoted the community of all human beings. His use of contrasts in this verse covers the full range of the most profound distinctions made within human society: racial or cultural, social or economic, sexual or gender-based (Witherington 2009). Paul does not intend these three divisions as comprehensive, but rather as illustrative. He is saying that, in Christ, all the barriers that divide one person from another are rendered null and void.

According to most Bible scholars, Paul's emphasis in this verse is not on abolishing gender differences, promulgating the *Magna Carta* of gender equality, or denying human categories generally (Botha 2000; Gundry-Volf 1997; Eisenbaum 2000; Witherington 2009). His concern is to show that neither being male nor being female is of any importance for being in Christ. As Gundry-Volf (1997) asserts, Paul has the "adiaphorization (this word comes from the Greek *adiaphora* for indifferent matters) of sex difference" in mind. This means that being male or female does not bring any advantage or disadvantage. Tolmie (2014) concurs that there is a deconstruction of the male hegemonic sentimentalities that pervaded the religio-socio-cultural contexts of Paul's time. The apostle re-prioritises ethnic, socio-economic and gender identities by subordinating them to "being in Christ". Every other distinction, including gender distinction, is subordinated to the Christian identity, which becomes the superior identity.

Thus, in Galatians 3:28, Paul's emphasis is on the transformation of social identities and social statuses of Christians rather than obliterating them. These ethnic, racial and social distinctions exist but they do not determine our functioning within the church of Christ or our interrelationships within the borderline of biblical principles. And the equal treatment of men and women in the church according to Galatians 3:28 is not hinged on being created in God's image (Genesis 1:26), but on their Christian identity.

In another vein, Neutel (2018) points out that in the light of first-century cosmopolitan ideals and worldviews, Paul's declaration of unity ("there is neither male nor female") takes on a distinctly ancient form. It does not proclaim the equality of all people, regardless of their social positions. Rather, it envisages a social ideal of harmony and connection, where those factors in society that create division and conflict have been removed.

The unity being projected by Paul in this text is not that of uniformity. Paul advocates for parity with respect to salvation, not a complete blurring of all human distinctions. He seeks to expunge the distinction which permits only qualified males to fulfill church roles (cf. 1 Timothy 2:12-14). Such distinction in the church would rebuild the wall that Jesus' redemptive work has pulled down. The fact that gender, social and racial distinctions continue to exist but do not determine functionality within ecclesial systems compels us to reorder our power structures. A complementary relationship between both sexes is established.

Theological implications of Galatians 3:28 for gender equality/equity in the church

Paul's theology in Galatians 3:28 calls for inclusiveness in ethnic, social and gender terms. With respect to gender, the arguments against women serving in positions of church leadership are similar to those presumably made by Paul's opponents to restrict leadership to Jewish believers only. He writes against the dominating gender construct of ethno-Jewish and Hellenistic-Roman society. Paul's understanding of salvation has implications for the church. In Christ, the old dualisms (Jew-Gentile, free-slave, male-female) are obliterated. Paul argues for a corporate identity that is geared towards social unity.

In Galatians 3:28, Paul affirms the negation of our distinctions on the basis of being a "new creature" (Galatians 6:15). But our individual differences in relation to gender (physical/biological) and social constitutions remain. Christians are to function in the church in expression of their spiritual gifting for the purpose of building up one another (cf. 1 Corinthians 12). The Holy Spirit is the common source behind the diversity of functions (1 Corinthians 12:4–7.11; see also Acts 2:16–18).

The actions that demean or subjugate women in church, either consciously or unconsciously, represent an intramural (*intra muros*) persecution, which Peters refers to as the most disturbing type of abuse because it is a persecution within the same body (2020:7). Patriarchal hierarchy puts obstacles in women's way, with the result that they cannot attain spiritual fulfillment nor express all of their God-given abilities. Among the many reasons for the persecution of the early church was that of identity. The early Christians were persecuted first for depicting a distinct identity from Judaism. This same problem of identity is at the crux of women's subjugation and persecution in the church.

As Uchem notes, "Nature has made male and female to be complementary and interdependent beings of the one human species, such that each is indispensable for the survival of humanity" (2005:49). Women and men in the church must collaborate to confront patriarchy and power monopoly in order for the global church to fulfill her divine mandate and mission in the world. Women and men are the two halves of the "body of Christ" and the world. Therefore, when women are denied leadership in the church and community, it results in the decapitation and crippling of the other half and so creates a dysfunctional body and dismembered world.

Jesus, the founder and head of the church, conferred equal dignity and personhood on women in a characteristically patriarchal society. He respected them, allowed them to speak publicly, acknowledged their faith, and accepted their support and help. Jesus' revolutionary treatment of women is clearly evident in his encounters with the Samaritan woman (John 4:1-26), the woman caught in adultery (John 8:3-11), and his teaching about equality in marriage (Matthew 19:1-12) and sexuality (Kohm 2008:352-353). This Christological template should be followed by the church. As Kohm states, "Christianity is consistent with the goal of gender equality" (2008:339). And Vorster (2019) affirms that "the equality of all people in Christ is the heart of all human relationships in the new covenant."

These theological evaluations of Galatians 3:28 have overarching implications. They call us to deconstruct concepts that characterize a dichotomy between males and females in their functionalities, and to eliminate the structures and expressions which associate power and superior leadership with everything male, while simultaneously associating weakness and perpetual followership with everything female. Our earthly identifiers should not create any value distinction between us. We should not use the specific ecclesial contexts of 1 Timothy 2:11-15 and Titus 2:4-5 to override a generalized ecclesial context indicated in Galatians 3:28. Paul affirms the full equality of men and women in ministry in other passages as well (1 Corinthians 11:5; 12:12-20; Romans 12:4-5.16; Colossians 3:15).

The church should strive consciously to describe gender relationships with holistic images that reaffirm that males and females are equal partners as a result of a common divine creation and common redemptive status. Also, patriarchal anthropology should be replaced with an inclusive theological anthropology, and gendered responsibilities should be replaced with partnering functionalities in the church and society. Men and women function differently in the Christian community, but no one should be limited in operation on the basis of their gender. Both sexes can serve equally in the ordained ministries of the church. There should be no exclusively male ministry.

Conclusion

Paul's assertion in Galatians 3:28 calls on the church to be dynamic and gender-inclusive in relation to the lived experiences of persecution suffered by women simply by virtue of being female within ecclesiastical contexts. Hence, there should be a rethinking of the biblical interpretation that projects women as inferior and as less than full persons. An integrative reading of Galatians 3:28, in line with the tapestry of the New Testament, affirms that all Christians are "one in Christ" and that all forms of distinctions count for nothing within the body of Christ. By implication, men and women are to mutually express their spiritual giftedness and opportunity for Christian ministry and service. And the church and the world are best served when men and women share responsibilities together as equal partners. Gender inequality and patriarchy is a barrier to the church's witness and the vocation of womanhood in our ecclesial and social communities, and it is a disruption of God's plan for the world. The church must consciously and intentionally entrench gender-transformative actions that promote gender equity, which invariably challenges patriarchy. Our theology of worship and ministry must match our theology of salvation.

Reflection Questions

1. What forms of persecution do women and girls face in our ecclesial contexts?

2. How can we achieve gender equity in the Church and society using biblical templates?

References

Ackerman, D. M. 1992. Defining our humanity: Thoughts on a feminist anthropology. *Journal of Theology for Southern Africa* 9, no. 79:13-23.

Aune, D. E. 2010. Galatians 3:28 and the problem of equality in the church and society. In P. Walters (eds.), *From Judaism to Christianity: Tradition and transition*. Leiden: Brill Publications, pp. 153-183.

Bird, Cliff and Seferosa Carroll. 2016. *Theology of gender equality*. Available at https://www.anglicancommunion.org/media/251166/Theology-of-Gender-Equality-PNG-April-2016.

Botha, Pieter. 2000. Submission and violence: Exploring gender relations in the first-century world. *Neotest* 34, no. 1: 1–38.

Casimir, Ani, Matthew Chukwuelobe and Collins Ugwu. 2014. The church and gender equality in Africa: Questioning culture and the theological paradigm on women oppression. *Open Journal of Philosophy* 4:166-173. Available at http://dx.doi.org/10.4236/ojpp.2014.42024.

Degner, S. C. 2001. *Biblical theology, exegesis of Galatians 3:28*. Available at http://www/wlstheologia.net/mode/37.

Dogo, Sefinatu. 2014. The Nigerian patriarchy: When and how. *Cultural and Religious Studies* 2, no. 5:263-275.

Donovan, Richard. 2016. Biblical commentary: Galatians 3:23-29. *Sermon Writer*. Available at https://www.sermonwriter.com/biblicalcommentary/galatians-323-29.

Eisenbaum, Pamela. 2000. Is Paul the father of misogyny and anti-Semitism? *Cross Currents* 50, no. 4: 506–24.

Esler, Philip. 2014. An outline of social identity theory. In: Brian Tucker and Coleman Barke (eds.), *The T & T Clark handbook to social identity in the New Testament*. New York: Bloomsbury T & T Clark, pp. 13–40.

Freedman, Jane. 2015. *Gendering the international asylum and refugee debate*. London: Palgrave Macmillan.

Grobler, Tommy. 2011. Neither male nor female: The implication of Galatians 3:26-29 for today's church. B.Th thesis, South African Theological Seminary, South Africa. Available at https://www.sats.eduza/wp-content/uploads/2014/09/Gend----T-Bachelors-Thesis-RES4361.pdf.

Gundry-Volf, Judith. 1997. Christ and gender: A study of difference and equality in Gal. 3, 28. In C. Landmesser, H. J. Eckstein and H. Lichtenberger (eds.), *Jesus Christus als die Mitte der Schrift. Studien zur Hermeneutik des Evangeliums*. New York: Walter de Groyter, pp. 439–77.

Heidebrecht, Doug. 2005. Distinction and function in the church: Reading Galatians 3:28 in context. *Direction Journal* 34, no. 2:181-193. Available at https://directionjournal.org/34/2/distinction-and-function-in-church.html.

Johnson, Lewis. 2005. Role distinctions in the church (Galatians 3:28). *Recovering Biblical Manhood and Womanhood*. Available at https://bible.org/seriespage/role-distinctions-church-galatians-328.

Kasomo, Daniel. 2010. The role of women in the church in Africa. *International Journal of Sociology and Anthropology* 2, no. 6:126-39.

Kelly, Nancy. 1993. Gender-related persecution: Assessing the asylum claims of women. *Cornell International Law Journal* 26, no. 3: 625–74.

Kohm, Lynne. 2008. A Christian perspective on gender equality. *Duke Journal of Gender Law & Policy* 15:339-63.

Lusey, Hendrew Et Al. 2017. Factors associated with gender equality among churchgoing young men in Kinshasa, Democratic Republic of Congo: A cross-sectional study. *International Journal for Equity in Health* 16, no. 213. Available at https://doi.org/10.1186/s12939_017-0707.7.

Mahendra, Shivray. 2016. The persecution of Christians in the world: Exploring a major trend in global Christianity. *New Life Theological Journal* 6, no. 2:33-45.

Martin, Ralph. 1979. Approaches to New Testament exegesis. In Howard Marshall (ed.), *New Testament interpretation: Essays on principles and methods*. Carlisle: The Paternoster Press, pp. 220-251.

Neutel, Karin. 2018. Galatians 3:28 – Neither Jew nor Greek, slave nor free, male and female. *Biblical Archaeology Review*. Available at https://www.biblicalarchaeology.org/daily/biblical-topics/bible-interpretation/galatians-3-28.

Peters, Prince. 2020. Understanding in Matthew 10:16-23 and its implication in the Nigerian church. *Theological Studies* 76(4). Available at https://doi.org/10.4102/hts-v76i45845.

Stamm, Richard. 1981. The Epistle to the Galatians: Introduction and exegesis. In G. A. Buttrick et al (eds.), *The Interpreter's Bible*. Nashville: Abingdon Press, pp. 518-20.

Tomie, Francois. 2014. Tendencies in the interpretation of Galatians 3:28 since 1990. *Acta Theologica* 19:105-29. Available at https://www.scielo.org.za/pdf/nt/v345/9/06.pdf.

Uchem, R. N. 2005. *Gender equality from a Christian perspective*. Enugu: SNAAP Press.

Van Huffel, Mary-Anne. 2011. Patriarchy as empire: A theological reflection. *Studia Historiae Ecclesiasticae* 37:259-70.

Vorster, Jakobus. 2019. The theological-ethical implications of Galatians 3:28 for a Christian perspective on perspective on equality as a foundational value in the human rights discourse. *In die Skriflig* 53(1). Available at https://doi.org/10.4102/ids.v53:1.2494.

Windsor, Lionel. 2002. *A history of interpretation of Galatians 3:28*. Available at www.Lionelwindsor.net/bibleresources/bible/new/Philip-Gal328-History-of-interpretation.pdf.

Witherington, Ben. 2009. *What's in the word: Rethinking the socio-rhetorical character of the New Testament*. Waco: Baylor University Press.

Wood, Hannelie. 2019. Gender inequality: The problem of harmful, patriarchal, traditional and cultural gender practices in the church. *Theological Studies* 75(1). Available at https://doi.org/10.4102/hts.v75i.1.5177.

More than Kindness – Jesus' Encounters with Women

Amanda Jackson

Introduction

In his time on earth, Jesus demonstrated that God's Kingdom is different to any other – fishermen would be leaders of his movement along with a tax collector (Matthew) and a political activist (Simon the Zealot). Followers would include a Roman centurion, a Samaritan leper and a woman unclean from bleeding, all people who would have been hated or despised by most Jews, but whom Jesus commended for their faith.[23]

In Jesus' interactions with all sorts of people, he challenged social expectations, popular beliefs and religious norms.[24]

Good news transforms

Jesus' first public teaching was a message of transformation. In the synagogue of Nazareth, he read from Isaiah, "The Spirit of the Lord is on me because he has anointed me to proclaim good news to the poor. He has sent me to proclaim freedom for the prisoners and recovery of sight for the

---

[23] When Jesus met the Roman centurion, he was amazed by his faith and told the crowds that the Kingdom of Heaven would have surprising subjects, "I say to you that many will come from the east and the west, and will take their places at the feast with Abraham, Isaac and Jacob in the kingdom of heaven. But the subjects of the kingdom will be thrown outside, into the darkness, where there will be weeping and gnashing of teeth."
The Samaritan leper is a double outsider as a foreigner and unclean with leprosy. In Luke 17:17-19 he is the only one of 10 lepers who praises God and thanks Jesus for his healing.
The woman with bleeding whom Jesus heals, had been suffering for 12 years and would have been considered unclean for all that time. Jesus calls her 'Daughter 'in Luke 8:48.

[24] In his letter to the church at Philippi, Paul echoes Jesus' example when he says that all his religious status as a Pharisee and all his social standing as a Roman citizen, count for nothing compared with 'the surpassing worth' of knowing Christ and having citizenship in heaven. Philippians 3:4-7; 20-21.

blind, to set the oppressed free, to proclaim the year of the Lord's favour." (Luke 4:18-19).

Everyone's eyes were on him, then he daringly claimed, "Today this scripture is fulfilled in your hearing." (v21)

So how is this transformational good news demonstrated in his interactions with women?

Most of us are aware that women in Jewish culture at the time of the New Testament were oppressed, second class members of society. They were valued only as daughters who could be married well, as wives who could produce male heirs and as domestic providers.

They were generally blamed by their community if they were childless, and that was one of many reasons men gave to justify divorcing their wives. They were seen as less reasoning than men and their word would not be believed unless ratified by a man.[25] How this had come to be for the gender specially created by God as *ezer kenegdo* - essential and equal to men[26] – has been discussed in other chapters. Essentially the partnership envisaged by God had been corrupted by sin and the power of men had led to physical, economic and sexual dominance.

Jesus was different. First of all he was gracious and kind to women who were poor or ostracised, like the generous poor widow in the Temple, or the frightened woman caught in adultery.[27] The fact that he even noticed such women was controversial.

But there was so much more than kindness in his attitude, words and actions. Jesus heralded a new Kingdom, reinstating God's original vision for men and women to be a partnership reflecting the image of God.[28]

Jesus and his mother Mary

A striking aspect of the coming of God into the world as a man is that his human mother plays such a significant role in pointing us to Jesus as Messiah. Mary's song about her unborn son, that comes at the beginning of

---

[25] A good summary of the ways Jesus broke with convention in his dealings with women can be found in Andrew Bartlett, *Men and Women in Christ, Fresh Light from the Biblical Texts*, IVP, 2019, p8.

[26] For an analysis of the translation of 'ezer' in Genesis 2 and elsewhere in the OT, see Marg Mowczko's 2010 blog, *A Suitable Helper* https://margmowczko.com/a-suitable-helper/ and Lucy Peppiatt, *Rediscovering Scripture's Vision for Women, Fresh Perspectives on Disputed Texts*, IVP, 2019, pp47-52.

[27] See Mark 12:43 and John 8:3-11.

[28] See Genesis 1:27, "God created human beings in His own image, in the image of God He created them; male and female he created them."

Luke's account, is a wonderful reminder from a young single girl of how God uses the lowly to bring about His purposes. She must know that falling pregnant in this strange way will be viewed as an affront to family honour[29] but she rejoices in God her Saviour.

> "From now on all nations will call me blessed
> For the Mighty One has done great things for me" (Luke 1:49)

Does that sound a little self-centred? It is actually an affirmation of her worth in God's Kingdom, an idea that will be seen again and again in the gospels in Jesus' encounters with women.[30]

But it is more than a song of personal rejoicing: Mary predicts the implications of the birth of her baby and reminds all generations about God's radical Kingdom.

> "He has performed mighty deeds with His arm;
> He has scattered the proud in their inmost thoughts.
> He has brought down rulers from their thrones
> but has lifted up the humble." (Luke 1:51-53)

A teenage girl is entrusted with deep truth.

Years later when Mary is distraught that her twelve year old son had gone missing in the big city of Jerusalem during Passover, she is chastised by Jesus for forgetting her prophetic insight and acting like a normal mum! He tells her she should have known to look for him in his Father's house.[31]

It must have been hard for Mary at times to be a mother to a boy showing more and more God-filled qualities. She pondered great truths and had spiritual insight but must have also been mystified by him.

Jesus loves his mother, and that is tenderly seen when, as he is dying on the cross, he asks John to look after her – "Here is your mother" and for her to take care of him – "Woman here is your son". We are told, "From that time on the disciple took her into his home." (John 19: 26-27)

---

[29] Carolyn Curtis James, Half the Church, Recapturing God's Global Vision for Women, Zondervan, 2011, pp144-145.

[30] It is interesting that Matthew also begins his gospel with a radical signifier that Jesus is different. His version of Jesus' genealogy – which would generally trace the father's heritage – mentions 5 women: Rahab, Tamar, Ruth, Bathsheba and Mary. And each of those women is an outsider.

[31] In the account in Luke Chapter 2, it's interesting that Jesus addresses his mother rather than his father when with slight exasperation, he dismisses their anxiety. "Why were you searching for me. Didn't you know I had to be in my Father's house?"

But it is disconcerting for his followers (and us) when on an earlier occasion, he seemed to dismiss his mother and brothers, who were waiting to see him. "'Who is my mother and who are my brothers?'[32] Pointing to his disciples, he said, 'Here are my mother and my brothers. For whoever does the will of my Father in heaven is my brother and sister and mother'" (Matthew 12:49). Putting aside the Jewish love of poetic exaggeration, this statement is establishing that in the Kingdom of God, family is an inclusive term for all followers, whatever their age, gender or status. And if he was pointing to his disciples when he mentioned sisters and brothers, there must have been women in the group as well as men. When Jesus took time to connect John and Mary at the cross as mother and son, he was connecting them as a spiritual family. They could guide and support each other equally at the church took root.

Pondering, questioning and wondering are definitely allowed by Jesus to grow faith. When Jesus began his public ministry, he went with his mother to a wedding in Cana. She tells the servants who have run out of wine, "Do whatever he tells you" (John 2:5), and in the first 'sign' of his glory, Jesus turned the water into wine of the highest quality. Presumably Mary is not surprised by this wedding celebration miracle but her understanding of the full significance of water and wine must have grown as she reflected on all she saw and heard over the coming years.

Jesus entrusting other women

The idea that Jesus should entrust not just his mother, but various other women, with significant truth about his purpose, death and kingdom is seen several times in the gospel accounts.

One instance is the meeting of Jesus and the Syro-Phoenician woman, a little story told in Matthew and Mark.[33] She is Greek, a foreigner, a pagan, who comes to him crying out for healing for her demon-possessed daughter, "Lord, son of David, have mercy on me!" Even though she has recognised him as Son of David or Messiah, Jesus ignores her, but when she follows after him, he tells her he has come only for the children of Israel. He compares foreigners to dogs, a harsh insult.[34]

---

[32] Craig Keener says that his statement would have been offensive to his hearers given that the 5th commandment was seen as so important and kinship ties were so highly valued. See *IVP Bible Background Commentary, New Testament*, Second Edition, IVP, 2014, p78.

[33] See Matthew 15 and Mark 7.

[34] *IVP Bible Background Commentary, New Testament*, Second Edition, IVP, 2014, p85.

His response sounds sharp and definitely off-putting but the translation may be unhelpful. The Greek term *kunaria* actually means 'little doggies.' Jesus is sharing a little joke with the woman, encouraging her in her faith. He shows her that he understands her world where there could be puppies under the table, unlike the Jewish households where dogs are excluded as they are unclean. His response is intended to show his sympathy with her and it stretches the crowd's understanding of foreigners being welcomed at the table.

Kneeling before him to show respect, she persists in calling on his healing help, arguing that even dogs eat crumbs form the master's table. She is implying that only a crumb of his power would be needed to heal her suffering daughter.

For such a clever response, Jesus praises her great faith, and heals her child.

Jesus took the time to engage with the woman and to dissect her understanding. Unlike the disciples who were caught in traditional cultural thinking and urged him to send her away (Matthew 15:23), Jesus engaged intellectually with a foreign woman – tackling a double dose of outsider status that baffled and angered onlookers.

Another un-named foreign woman of dubious repute is the Samaritan whom Jesus encounters at the well in Sychar. We see him take the time in the hot sun (20 verses of John 4 are devoted to her) to engage with her and challenge her understanding of salvation. As a result, many in her village are brought to faith in "the Saviour of the world". She has rightly been called the first evangelist.[35]

What an amazing discussion it is, similar to the probing exchange between Jesus and Nicodemus. But he is a Pharisee with status and learning while she is a despised Samaritan village woman. Jesus explores ideas on living water and true worship with her as an equal[36] and reveals to her that he is the Messiah (John 4:26).

She believes; and calls her fellow villagers to meet the man who "told me everything I ever did" (v39). Because of that compelling testimony, many believed and Jesus was asked to stay two days in the village. I wonder how many future church planters came from Sychar.

---

[35] See for example, National Catholic Reporter, https://www.ncronline.org/blogs/simply-spirit/clueless-preaching-about-samaritan-woman-misses-point.

[36] Craig Keener in the IVP Bible Background Commentary on verse 27 notes that traditional Jewish piety warned men not to talk much with women, even their own wife, because of temptation and even because observers might assume misconduct. Traditional Greek and Roman culture also considered it inappropriate for a wife to talk with men in an unguarded setting. Op cit, p260.

The story of the woman is interesting in many ways: when I was younger, the main point about the woman seemed to be that she had had five husbands and was therefore a sinner, guilty of the worst sort of failing – sexual sin[37]. It is positive that now, the woman is seen more as a witness and evangelist.

Jesus is less interested in her lifestyle than in opening up for her the radical good news that she could worship Jesus as saviour of the world. He certainly does not overlook her many husbands, but once he has commented (v18), he considers it much more important to discuss theological truth with her. Why didn't he seek out the male village leaders? Is he showing that his water is available for everyone?

He knows she is ready to receive truth – and indeed she seems better able to understand Jesus' metaphor of living water than the disciples can grasp the figurative idea of the food of life (see v32-33). She witnesses to her village that Jesus could be the Messiah (v29) and many of them discover that truth for themselves because Jesus amazingly stays with them several days.

John is the only gospel writer to tell us of the wedding at Cana and the woman at the well – stories rich in symbolism that show how ready he is to reveal deep truth to ordinary women. And they shared that truth – proclaiming and teaching.

Even Jesus' closest followers learn and grow as they grapple with Kingdom ideas. Peter is the famous example of impetuous faith on one page and failure on the next.

Jesus deepening women's faith

We know and recognise this – and take comfort in his humanity – but we have taken less note of that same journey of deepening faith taken by key women in Jesus' entourage. Of the disciples who are named in the gospels, a number are women – Mary Magdalen, Joanna (the wife of the manager of Herod's household), Susanna, Mary (mother of James and Joseph),

---

[37] The assumption was that the woman was of dubious honour if she had had 6 different relationships with men. But Jesus seems more interested in showing her that she doesn't need to seek security in men who will exploit her and then abandon her – she has access to the living water of salvation. It is interesting that the account in John does not actually record the woman's response to Jesus's claim to be the Messiah, see v26: maybe the coming of the disciples in v 27 stopped her from responding. But it is clear she was transformed. For a discussion of this interpretation of the story, see Grady J. Lee, *Fearless Daughters of the Bible*, Chosen Publishing, 2012, Ch 12.

Salome, Martha, Mary of Bethany. Amongst Jesus' followers, Luke notes that 'many' women supported Jesus and were taught by him (Luke 8:3).[38]

Let us look at how the sisters Martha and Mary of Bethany find deeper faith and understanding.

The famous story (Luke 10:38-42) that introduces the women takes place in their home, where Martha is the head of a household of siblings[39]. Mary is cast as the younger and perhaps less practical sister and Martha as the responsible older sister, distracted by her domestic responsibilities.

It is a great story to emphasise the importance of taking time to learn at the feet of Jesus. Mary is welcomed by Jesus to learn, to be a disciple, while he gently chides Martha that being stressed about providing hospitality (a classic female role in any home) is not as important as taking the chance to learn.

But just as important to our understanding of the character of Martha and Mary is the description of the sickness and death of their younger brother, Lazarus (See John 11:1-44).

Martha and Mary call for Jesus to come when their brother falls ill. But strangely, he waits two days to go Bethany, even though John tells us that Jesus loved the family. It is a sign so that people may believe.

Before Jesus arrives, Martha goes to meet Jesus outside the village. Even at this time of great sadness, Jesus encourages Martha in her grasp of life, death and resurrection. Martha proclaims, "I believe that you are the Messiah, the Son of God." She uses exactly the same words as Peter used when he was questioned by Jesus.

What an amazing confession of faith in the midst of her great grief. She has certainly been listening and learning since the evening when Jesus came to her home. Mary too, falls at Jesus' feet and asserts that Lazarus would not have died if Jesus had been with him.

Martha and Mary must have accompanied Jesus on his travels and been taught as part of the group of close followers.

Women learning with men: why would Jesus have encouraged the participation of 'many women' in his group of followers AND been prepared to put up with negative responses, if he were not establishing a model for the Church?

---

[38] For a full discussion of Jesus' women followers, see Marg Mowczko's theology blog from 2014, *Jesus had many female followers - many!* https://margmowczko.com/many-women-followed-jesus-gospels/.

[39] Martha is always mentioned first and no husbands are mentioned so it fair to assume that the sisters were either single or widowed. Lazarus does not feature in Luke 10 but is described as a close friend in John 11.

Martha declared to her Teacher, "God will give you whatever you ask", and He did! She must have taken a further stride in faith witnessing the miracle of her brother coming back to life.

Not long after, Mary anointed Jesus' feet with expensive perfume and wiped his feet with her hair. "And the house was filled with the fragrance of the perfume" (John 12:3). It is clearly an act of extravagant worship, preparing Jesus for his death, that would come only a week later[40].

There are three different incidents where women anoint Jesus with perfume or tears[41] and we should not ignore these stories of intimacy and love. Jesus was not annoyed or embarrassed by Mary's action, nor by the other women. Male witnesses tended to be cross or indignant at the waste of money or the dubious character of the women but Jesus praises their love and the symbolic insight of the deed. Without speaking, the women signal that they understand Jesus' identity and mission. And by highlighting the cost of the perfume – a year's wages – the writers show the that the cost of discipleship is high, but worth it.

Surely Jesus' view of women should guide us today – to appreciate women for their gifting, their ability to declare truth, and to teach lessons of faith from a place of brokenness. Few women in the Bible have the chance to be arrogant (!) because they lack power, so they are well placed to show meekness and humility. And perhaps they can worship more easily in spirit and truth, with divine insight. Jesus interacted with the individual depending on where they are at. He cried, became angry and also debated holy texts.

The account of a woman anointing Jesus at the home of Simon the Leper (recounted in both Matthew and Mark) shows Jesus' blessing of instinctive faith. She pours a whole jar of expensive perfume called nard over his head, an action that is called "a beautiful thing"[42]. But more than that, Jesus says that "wherever the gospel is preached throughout the world, what she has done will also be told." It is a humble and generous act of service but is that all that Jesus is noticing? We should 'preach' about the woman because she recognises in a deep part of her being that Jesus is going to his death and she is preparing his body for burial. She "did what she could" to worship, when others too easily would walk away from his arrest and death.

---

[40] Grady J Lee, Fearless Daughters of the Bible, p170.
[41] In Matthew 26 and Mark 14, an unnamed woman anoints Jesus' head with expensive perfume in Bethany. In Luke 7, an unnamed woman anoints Jesus' feet with her teas and with perfume and in John 12, Mary, Martha's sister anoints Jesus' feet with perfume. There are similarities in all the accounts but also differences.
[42] The accounts are in Matthew 26:6-13 and Mark 14:3-9.

In Luke's gospel, "a sinful woman" anoints Jesus' feet with her tears, wipes them with her hair, kisses them and pours perfume over them. Jesus says her faith has saved her, which shocks the Pharisees. Sexual impurity which has been a strong barrier for women in cultures throughout history, is set aside by Jesus in favour of genuine care and acceptance. The emphasis is on her tears and great love which are matched by Jesus' forgiveness. Again we see instinctive spiritual worship.

The woman with haemorraging was unclean and thus prevented from worshipping in the Temple: Jesus freed her to be a daughter of God. The sinful woman in Luke is set free to be a forgiven worshipper and the woman caught in adultery whom the Pharisees want to stone, is freed from the hypocrisy of their condemnation.[43]

Jesus' death and resurrection witnessed by women

Finally, we see the importance of women in the accounts of Jesus' death and resurrection, the culmination of his earthly ministry. The eye-witness evidence of women is crucial to establishing that Jesus has risen from the dead. Yet, in Jewish society at the time, women could not give formal evidence[44] and their opinions were generally treated dismissively. Why would God bother to tell His most vital news using women's voices unless He is emphasising the equal worth of men and women to telling the good news of the Kingdom?

Let's look at the accounts. All four gospels highlight the importance of women as witnesses at the cross and at the tomb. Matthew tells us "many women were there" at the cross and he names women who must have been well known: Mary Magdalene, Mary mother of James and Joseph and the mother of Zebedee's sons. Mark also tells us that female followers watched the crucifixion, and to the list of names adds Salome. These were not just curious onlookers – Mark and Luke both mention that the women had travelled from Galilee with Jesus and cared for his needs. Mark says, "Many other women who had come up with him to Jerusalem were also there." That description is a reminder that Jesus was an unusual, even scandalous teacher – the norm was male-only followers.[45]

---

[43] NT Wright says that the story of 'the woman caught in adultery' would be better called, 'the men caught in hypocrisy'. NT Wright and Michael F Bird, The New Testament In Its World, An Introduction to the History, Literature and Theology of the First Christians, SPCK, 2019, p669.
[44] See https://www.torahinmotion.org/discussions-and-blogs/shevuot-30-a-woman-dayan. Also note Andrew Bartlett's comments referred to in Footnote 3.
[45] Craig S Keener, op cit, p123.

The women had roles as patrons, helpers and disciples but at the cross it is their grief and weeping that are described. Such emotion could be considered simply a customary feminine response were it not for the fact that Luke tells us of Jesus' empathy for the mothers of Jerusalem in coming persecution. In the midst of his suffering for the salvation of the world, Jesus turns to the women, "Daughters of Jerusalem, do not weep for me, weep for yourselves and for your children" (Luke 23:28). It is a sobering reminder that women through the ages bear the pain of violence for their gender and faith.[46]

On the morning after the Sabbath, women go to the tomb to anoint Jesus' body. All four gospel accounts describe how they are the first witnesses to the resurrection[47]. Five are named among others – Mary Magdalene, Mary the mother of James, Salome, the other Mary and Joanna – their stories must have been repeated many times over the next years. They were frightened by an angel who told them, "He has risen!" At first the disciples did not believe the women's report.

Mary Magdalene's personal encounter with Jesus[48] shows us again how willing Jesus was to engage with women as equals, as friends, as messengers of truth. It is an intimate scene: Mary is crying and does not recognise Jesus until he calls her name. He entrusts her to pass on news about what she has seen but also about his spiritual condition (he has not yet ascended) and ends with a remarkable affirmation of Mary's status as a sister believer, "I am ascending to my Father and your Father, to my God and your God." This is a woman who has been released from seven demons – we are not told how they affected her but they must have led to shame, self hatred and perhaps abuse[49]. Everyone knows her past but also that she is a new woman. She has been completely transformed and is given the task of telling the disciples of her encounter with the risen Lord and all he had said to her.[50]

---

[46] Fascinating research by Open Doors International shows the hidden double impact of violence against women – for their faith and because they are women. See their 2020 report https://www.opendoorsuk.org/news/latest-news/hidden-persecution-report.

[47] Andrew Bartlett, op cit, p309.

[48] John and Mark describe Mary Magdalene meeting Jesus alone; Matthew writes that a group of women met Jesus as they hurried away from the tomb, 'came to him, clasped his feet and worshipped him.'

[49] Grady J Lee, op cit, p193.

[50] Anne Graham Lotz, the daughter of Billy Graham and a gifted Bible teacher in her generation has spoken of Mary Magdalene as "commissioned to go to men to share her testimony and also to give his Word." Quoted in https://www.baptist

What an amazing culmination to the gospel story, that women were entrusted with the vital news, "He has risen". It is not a competition between men and women over who was first to know or who is more important; it is a wonderful balance of male and female responses to the news that reflects God's design of male and female.

In the upper room the Holy Spirit comes at Pentecost to the 120 'brother and sisters' (Acts 1:15) who are gathered, including Mary the mother of Jesus. Peter quotes from the prophet Joel, "Even on my servants, both men and women, I will pour out my Spirit in those days."

Jesus noticed women, he restored them, he took them seriously, he taught them and he entrusted them with truth. His life and ministry on earth brought in a Kingdom to release us all to use our spiritual gifting, men and women alongside each other, set free from cultural barriers and spiritual bondage.

There is still a challenge and opportunity for us today – are we dampening our effectiveness as the church by limiting the service and leadership of women?

Reflection Questions

1. How do you see this chapter on the gospels linking with earlier chapters on God's character and plan for men and women?

2. Jesus has interactions with many women and this chapter points out that their discussions were sometimes searching discussions of theology. Why is that important as we think about roles and relationships for women and men in our churches today?

---

press.com/resource-library/news/60-minutes-segment-on-anne-graham-lotz-muddied-sbc-stance-on-women-in-ministry/.

Women and Men and Ministry in First-Century Churches

Margaret Mowczko

Introduction

For most of the church's history, and in most Christian movements and denominations, only men have been permitted to serve as official ministers and leaders in churches. Some women have served in recognized positions but usually with more restrictions and fewer responsibilities than men. Furthermore, their responsibilities have typically been limited to women and children. But it has not always been this way.

In the pages of the New Testament, we see that both men and women cared for local churches, and both men and women were missionaries and evangelists. These ministers often braved hardships and dangers in order to protect congregations and in order to spread the message of Jesus in a world that could be suspicious and hostile towards new religious ideas.

In this chapter I look at some of the women mentioned in the book of Acts and in Paul's New Testament letters, highlighting their participation in the first-century apostolic church. My aim is to demonstrate that some women were prominent members of their churches. I will further show that women, as well as men, and often *with* men, were leaders in congregations and in missions. I also discuss Paul's theology of ministry and his words in 1 Timothy 2:11-15. 1 Timothy 2:12, in particular, is a verse that is often understood as prohibiting women from teaching and leading men. Did Paul limit the ministry of women?

I. Many women!

From the very beginning of the Christian movement, women probably outnumbered men. The Synoptic Gospels tell us that many women followed Jesus around Galilee during his ministry. Many also followed him to Jerusalem where they watched his crucifixion (e.g., Mt 27:55-56; Mk 15:40-41). Women were devoted to Jesus and many sponsored his ministry with their own money (Lk 8:1-3). In the birth and passion narratives, especially, we see that women were with Jesus from his birth to his death and resurrection, and they cared for him and served him in a manner not described of the male disciples.

After Jesus's ascension, women were with the Twelve and with Jesus's brothers praying in the upper room (Acts 1:13-14). Mary the mother of Jesus was there and other women who probably included Mary Magdalene, Joanna, Susanna, Salome, and several other Marys. In Acts 1:15, we are told of a gathering where about 120 believers met together. Possibly half of these 120 were women. If information from early church documents as well as church statistics from more recent centuries are any indication, however, there would have been more women than men. This gives us the rough figure of sixty-plus female followers of Jesus in Jerusalem at this point in time.

A few days later, on the day of Pentecost, the believers were together again when the Holy Spirit was poured out. In his speech given on that momentous day, Peter quotes from the prophet Joel and he mentions women as well as men.

> And in the last days, God says, 'I will pour out my Spirit on all people.
> And your sons and your daughters will prophesy,
> And your youth will see visions and your seniors will dream dreams.
> And indeed on my male servants and on my female servants I will pour out
> my Spirit in those days, and they will prophesy.'
> Acts 2:17-18 (own translation)

Women and men received the empowering of the Holy Spirit and were witnesses of the birth of the church at Pentecost.

II. Women and men as hosts of house churches (overseers)

Women were not a small or marginalized group among the first Christians. Still, the church in Jerusalem seems to have been primarily led by men. The author of Acts, traditionally thought to be Luke, mentions the twelve apostles by name in Acts 1. Peter, who ministers with John, is the focus of the narratives in Acts chapters 2-5 while the other apostles are referred to more generally and as a group. (After Acts 1, most of the Twelve are never mentioned by name again in the New Testament.) The twelve male apostles were proclaiming the gospel, teaching new believers, healing people, and performing miracles. They were meeting daily with the community of believers in the temple courts and in homes (Acts 2:46; 5:42).⁵¹ Then in Acts 6, seven men are chosen to minister to the Greek-speaking widows. What were the women doing?

Luke tells the stories of only some people in the Jerusalem church. He does not tell us about the activities of Mary the mother of Jesus or of Mary Magdalene or Joanna, for example, yet we can assume these women were doing at least some of the same things that the men were doing. In Acts 12, however, Luke does tell us that when Peter was released from prison he went directly to the house of a woman, Mary of Jerusalem.

Mary of Jerusalem

As well as being the mother of a minister (John Mark) and the aunt of a minister (Barnabas), Mary was involved in ministry herself. She held church meetings in her own home in Jerusalem. Acts 12 tells us that despite the threat of persecution—Herod Agrippa had killed James and imprisoned Peter—she held a prayer meeting.

Up until the 300s, there were practically no church buildings, so providing a home base for a congregation was a vital ministry. Most congregations in the first century were house-churches and they were not large, consisting of between a dozen to sixty members. Relatively wealthy believers opened their homes and cared for the physical and spiritual well-being of congregations. They also opened their homes to visiting apostles, prophets, teachers and other ministers who brought words of encouragement and instruction, as well as news from other churches.⁵² Several women and men mentioned in the New Testament hosted and cared for congregations in their homes. Some scholars believe these people were the first church overseers (Greek: *episkopoi*).⁵³

---

51 Some argue that because the Twelve were all men, women cannot be church leaders. I discuss this idea on my website. https://margmowczko.com/the-twelve-apostles-were-all-male/.
52 The lady and her congregation (literally, 'her children') who receive the letter known as 2 John are warned not to host ministers who bring unsound teaching (2 John 1:10). See my article, *The Elder and the Lady: A Look at the Language of Second John*. https://margmowczko.com/elder-lady-language-2-john/
53 For example, in a discussion on 1 Timothy 3, Kevin Giles writes, 'The argument that the bishops [*episkopoi*] and deacons are house-church leaders is now the prevailing scholarly consensus'. Giles, *Patterns of Ministry among the First Christians* (Eugene OR: Cascade Books, 2017), 61.
Most *episkopoi* were men, and Paul's words in 1 Timothy 3:1-7 reflect this.

We do not hear much about the women of the church in Jerusalem or in Judea, or in nearby provinces. Still, we know women were ministering as hosts: Mary in Jerusalem; as carers of widows and the poor: Tabitha in Joppa (Acts 9:36-42); as prophets: Philip's daughters in Caesarea Maritima (Acts 21:9). We hear even less about the women in Syrian Antioch. But as we move northwest from Syria—to the Roman provinces of Asia, Macedonia, Achaia, and to Rome itself—the names of women are mentioned in the New Testament in increasing numbers. Most of these women were associated with the apostle Paul. One of them is Lydia.

Lydia in Philippi

Lydia was a gentile woman but also an adherent to Judaism. She was in a Jewish prayer-house in the Macedonian city of Philippi when Paul and his team turned up and brought the message of Jesus. Luke records that 'The Lord opened her heart to respond to Paul's message' (Acts 16:14). She was Paul's first convert in Europe.

Lydia was a dealer of expensive purple fabric, a luxury product, and she appears to have had a relatively spacious home. After she and her household were baptized, Lydia hosted Paul and his team. It seems she also hosted the Philippian church in her home, as Paul and Silas encouraged the brothers and sisters in Lydia's home before they moved on to the next city to carry on their mission (Acts 16:40). Lydia is the only Philippian identified by name in Acts 16, indicating that she played a significant role in the church, most likely continuing her role as the host of the first Philippian congregation.

What might the women and men who hosted first-century churches have done? Margaret Y. MacDonald comments on gatherings in Roman homes, including church meetings.

> In the Roman world, it was normal procedure for the person in whose house a group met to preside, select the meal, and organize the entertainment to follow, which could include a visiting philosopher or wisdom figure. It is reasonable to conclude that women such as Lydia in Philippi and Phoebe in Cenchreae were presiding in their homes as they entertained Paul and his fellow workers.[54]

However, none of the qualifications in these verses in the Greek text states that *only* men are permitted to be *episkopoi*.

[54] Margaret Y. MacDonald, 'The Religious Lives of Women in the Early Christianity', *Women's Bible Commentary*, Third Edition, Carol A. Newsom, Sharon H. Ringe,

We look at Phoebe in the following section.

III. Women and men in Christian service (ministers and deacons)

Jesus did not give his followers a precise plan on how they should organize themselves for worship or for missions. Rather than leaving a set of rules about leadership structures in the church, he gave guiding principles about relationships among his followers. One of these principles was a warning against emulating the kind of leadership that has been typical throughout much of the world's history. Jesus commissioned his followers to be servants and not masters or rulers (e.g., Mk 10:42-44; Lk 22:24-27; Jn 13:3-15). Jesus himself provided the example of 'the one who serves' (*ho diakonōn*) (Lk 22:27).

Following on from Jesus's example and his teachings, Paul also emphasized that the community of Christian believers was to be led and ministered to by servants (e.g., 1 Cor 3:5; 4:1). In accordance with this idea, Paul often uses the Greek nouns *diakonos* ('servant/ minister') and *diakonia* ('service/ ministry'), and the verb *diakoneō* ('serve/ minister'). He only uses these words for ministers and ministry; he never uses them for ordinary servants.

Paul typically used the word *diakonos* with the sense of an 'agent with a sacred commission.'[55] As such, several *diakonoi* (plural) are described as being a *diakonos* of Christ (1 Tim 4:6), or of God (e.g. 2 Cor 6:4), or of the gospel (Eph 3:7), or of a church—a church being a sacred community of 'saints' (Ro 16:1-2). Apart from three exceptions, Paul used *diakonos* as a term for Christian ministers or agents.[56] These *diakonoi* include Paul himself (Ro 15:25; 1 Cor 3:5; Eph 3:7; Col 1:23, etc), Timothy (1 Tim 4:6), Epaphras (Col 1:7), Tychicus (Eph 6:21-22; Col 4:7-9), Apollos (1 Cor 3:5), and even Jesus Christ (Ro 15:8). He also referred to a woman, Phoebe, as a *diakonos*. She was a *diakonos*, or deacon, of the church at Cenchreae in Corinth.

Jacqueline E. Lapsley (eds) (Louisville, KY: Westminster John Knox Press, 2012), 640-647, 642.

[55] See the work of John N. Collins who has written several books and papers on *diakon-* words noting their implicit sense of agency. For example, Collins, *Diakonia: Reinterpreting the Ancient Sources* (Oxford: Oxford University Press, 1990).

[56] In Romans 13:1-5 Paul refers to Roman governing authority with the word *diakonos*. Roman rule was not at all Christian, yet is described by Paul as 'God's agent (*diakonos*) for your good' (Ro 13:4). Note also Paul's description of false apostles as agents (*diakonoi*) of Satan with a diabolic commission (2 Cor 11:13-15). And in Galatians 2:17 Paul asks the rhetorical question if Jesus is an agent (*diakonos*) of sin.

Phoebe of Cenchrea

When writing to the Romans, Paul introduces Phoebe to them.

> I commend to you Phoebe, our sister, who is a minister (diakonos) of the church at Cenchreae, so that you may welcome her in the Lord as is appropriate for saints, and help her in whatever she needs from you, for she has been a patron of many and of myself. Romans 16:1-2 (own translation)

Some English translations call Phoebe a servant rather than a minister or deacon, but she could not have been a servant in the usual sense of the word. We know this because Paul also describes her as a 'patron of many'. As a patron, Phoebe would have had wealth, and wealthy women were not servants, they had servants of their own. Phoebe also had clout. Patronage was a social system that was pervasive in the first-century Roman world, and patrons, whether men or women, were influential people.[57] Through patronage, women 'won for themselves liberty to speak and act in political and religious affairs'.[58]

As well as being a minister in her church and a patron, it is widely accepted that Phoebe travelled from Cenchreae as Paul's envoy and delivered his letter to the Christians in Rome. In this role, she would have passed on news about Paul and answered questions that arose when his letter was read aloud to the original audience. Perhaps she was the one who first read Paul's letter aloud to the Romans. Whatever the case, Phoebe was a minister who was commended and trusted by Paul.

---

[57] The practice of patronage was informal and voluntary, but there were certain social constraints and reciprocal obligations involving the client-patron relationship. These constraints and obligations were an extension of the honour-shame dynamic that pervaded Greco-Roman society, and the typical client-patron relationship was one of unequal power. A wealthy man or woman who made a generous donation to his or her city, community, guild, or to an individual, etc., was able to exercise considerable influence and power. Patrons expected loyalty, public support, as well as public praise that reinforced or elevated the patron's level of honour. In Christian communities, some of these dynamics would have been tempered, but patrons still had clout. See Carolyn Osiek, 'Diakonos and Prostatis: Women's Patronage in Early Christianity', HTS Theological Studies 61 (1 & 2) (2005): 346-370.

[58] Greg W. Forbes and Scott D. Harrower, Raised from Obscurity: A Narrative and Theological Study of the Characterization of Women in Luke-Acts (Eugene, OR: Wipf and Stock, 2015), 32.

IV. Women and men in partnership with Paul (coworkers)

The apostle Paul was all about partnership. He rarely ministered on his own but travelled and served with fellow ministers whom he sometimes calls coworkers. He wrote his letters with others, with people whom he lists as co-authors or co-senders. He fostered relationships between churches and within churches. Paul understood that the Christian life is about partnership, or sharing, with each other in community, and he was keenly concerned with how Christians related to and ministered to each other.

Unlike what we see in many congregational meetings today, Paul encouraged church members to participate in vocal ministry, even spontaneously, as long as it wasn't done in a selfish, disorderly, or unedifying manner.[59]

To the church in Corinth, Paul wrote,

> What then, brothers and sisters? Whenever you come together, each one has a hymn, a teaching, a revelation, a tongue, or an interpretation. Everything is to be done for building up. 1Cor 14:26 (CSB)

To the church in Colossae, he wrote,

> Let the word of Christ dwell richly among you, in all wisdom teaching and admonishing one another through psalms, hymns, and spiritual songs, singing to God with gratitude in your hearts. Colossians 3:16 (CSB)

Women and men participated in ministry in many of the churches Paul founded or took an active interest in. This is especially clear in the last chapter of Romans, where Paul asks that certain people be greeted.

In Romans 16:3-16, straight after Phoebe of Cenchreae's commendation, twenty-eight Roman Christians are mentioned, and at least nine of these are women. Considering the culture of the time and that many women had fewer social freedoms than men, nine is a considerable number. What is more noteworthy, however, is that more women in the list of twenty-eight are described by, or commended for, their ministries than men: six Roman women (Prisca, Mary, Junia, Tryphena, Tryphosa, Persis)

---

[59] In 1 Corinthians 14:26-40, Paul silences three groups of people in the church at Corinth, including women who wanted to learn, because their speech was unruly and unedifying. He did not silence men and women who prayed, prophesied, and ministered in an edifying manner (cf. 1 Cor 11:5).

compared with three men (Aquila, Andronicus, Urbanus). And two of these men are ministering alongside a female partner (Aquila with Prisca, Andronicus with Junia). Moreover, Prisca is mentioned first of the twenty-eight Roman Christians. First!

Prisca and Aquila

Prisca, also known as Priscilla, is mentioned before her husband Aquila four of the six times the couple are named in (most) Greek texts of the New Testament.[60] Prisca and Aquila were friends of Paul. The three had lived, worked, travelled, and ministered together, and Paul refers to them with his favourite ministry term, coworkers.[61] The couple also ministered when they were apart from their friend. When Paul, writing from Rome, closes his second letter to Timothy who was in Ephesus, Prisca is again greeted first before her husband as well as before the household of Onesiphorus (2 Tim 4:19). (No other Christians, apart from Timothy, are greeted in 2 Timothy.) By listing Prisca first, Paul is highlighting her prominence in ministry.

Prisca and Aquila hosted and cared for a church in Ephesus (1 Cor 16:19, cf. 16:8) and, later, a church in Rome (Ro 16:3-5a). Luke records that when the couple was in Ephesus, they were the ones who corrected the doctrine of the visiting teacher Apollos. That Luke includes this story in Acts indicates that the event was significant. Furthermore, he does not express the slightest discomfort or concern when reporting that Priscilla, a woman, with her husband Aquila 'explained the word of God *more accurately*' to a man who is described as having a thorough knowledge of the scriptures and who was teaching *accurately* about Jesus. (See Acts 18:24-26.)

As well as Prisca and Aquila, Paul identifies several more men and women as his coworkers: Urbanus (Ro 16:9); Timothy (Ro 16:21); Titus

---

[60] The couple is named in Acts 18:2.18.26, Romans 16:3-5, 1 Corinthians 16:19, and 2 Timothy 4:19. Unlike other ancient Greek texts of Acts, the fifth-century Codex Bezae has Aquila's name first and Priscilla's second in Acts 18:26. This order of names was adopted in Acts 18:26 of Stephanus's sixteenth-century Greek text which was used by the translators of the King James Bible. In the King James Bible, Prisca is mentioned before her husband three times.

[61] Edward Earle Ellis has observed, 'The designations most often given to Paul's fellow workers are in descending order of frequency as follows: coworker (*synergos*), brother (*adelphos*) [or sister (*adelphē*) as in the cases of Phoebe and Apphia], minister (*diakonos*) and apostle (*apostolos*).' Ellis, 'Paul and his Coworkers', *Dictionary of Paul and His Letters*, Gerald Hawthorne and Ralph Martin (ed) (Downers Grove, IL: InterVarsity Press, 1993), 183.

(2 Cor 8:23); Epaphroditus (Phil 2:25) Euodia, Syntyche, and Clement (Phil 4:2-3); Aristarchus, Mark, and Justus (Col 4:10-11); Philemon (Phlm 1); Mark, Aristarchus, Demas, and Luke (Phlm 24). We look at Euodia and Syntyche next.

Euodia and Syntyche in Philippi

Paul names Euodia and Syntyche in his letter to the Philippians and gives us a glimpse into the importance of their ministries.

> I urge Euodia and I urge Syntyche to think the same thing in the Lord. Indeed, I ask you, my true partner, to help these women who have contended together with me in the gospel, along with Clement and the rest of my coworkers, whose names are in the book of life.
> Philippians 4:2-3 (Own translation)

These two women were prominent and influential in the Philippian church; otherwise, Paul would not have taken the trouble to address each of them directly in this letter. Earlier in Philippians, he had mentioned that Timothy had served with him 'in the gospel' and here he says that Euodia and Syntyche where involved with him 'in the gospel.' Furthermore, Paul uses a strong word when he says they 'contended together' (*synathleō*) with him. In their definition of *synathleō*, BDAG explain that by using this word, Paul is saying the women had fought bravely at his side in spreading the gospel.[62] Theirs was not a lightweight or trivial ministry, and Paul appeals to his 'true partner', which may refer to the church at Philippi, to assist the women.[63] Paul similarly asked the church in Rome to help Phoebe in her ministry (Ro 16:2).

Some scholars are reluctant to acknowledge that Euodia and Syntyche were leaders. However, Gordon D. Fee, among others, understands that Euodia and Syntyche were indeed 'leaders in the believing community at Philippi.'[64] Centuries earlier, Chrysostom stated, 'These women seem to me to be the chief (*to kephalaion*) of the church' in Philippi (Homily 13 on

---

[62] Walter Bauer, *A Greek-English Lexicon of the New Testament and Other Early Christian Literature*, Third Edition, revised and edited by F.W Danker, s.v. συναθλέω (Chicago: University of Chicago Press, 2000), 964. This lexicon is known as BDAG, an acronym of the surnames of the four editors who have worked on it since the first edition.

[63] See Richard G. Fellows and Alistair C. Stewart: "Euodia and Syntyche and the Role of Syzygos: Phil 4:2-3" *ZNW* 109.2 (2018): 222-234.

[64] Gordon D. Fee, *Paul's Letter to the Philippians* (The New International Commentary on the New Testament; Eerdmans: Grand Rapids, 1995), 389.

Philippians). Euodia and Syntyche, like other first-century women and men, worked hard in gospel ministry as leaders, and Paul approved.[65]

V. Women and men in difficult, dangerous ministries (labourers and apostles)

Being a Christian in the first century could be difficult and dangerous. There was often suspicion, alienation, and even persecution from family, friends, and the community when someone rejected their traditional customs, Jewish or pagan, to follow Jesus. It could be even more difficult for ministers. Reflecting this hardship, Paul uses the word "labour" (verb: *kopiaō*; noun: *kopos*) several times in his letters in the context of his evangelistic and apostolic ministry (1 Cor 3:8; 15:10; Gal 4:11; Phil 2:16; Col 1:29; 1 Thess 3:5).

Paul also used the word 'labour' in reference to local leadership ministries. For example,

> Now we ask you, brothers and sisters, to acknowledge those who labour (kopiaō) among you, who lead/care (proistēmi) for you in the Lord, and who advise you. Hold them in the highest regard in love because of their work.
> 1 Thessalonians 5:12-13a (own translation. cf. 1 Tim 5:17; 1 Cor 16:16).

While he occasionally used *kop-* words in the context of ordinary manual labour (1 Cor 4:12; 1 Thess 2:9; 2 Thess 3:8), in most other contexts Paul is referring to Christian ministry.

Mary of Rome, Tryphaena, Tryphosa, and Persis

Paul identifies four women in Romans 16 using 'labour' words: Mary, Tryphaena, Tryphosa, and Persis.

---

[65] Paul encouraged each woman to, literally, 'think the same thing in the Lord.' He used similar language when he urged all the Philippians, literally, 'that you (plural) may think the same thing' (Phil 2:2). This phrase is part of one long sentence (2:1-4) which is followed by 2:5 where Paul tells the Philippians to think like Jesus, that is, have the same attitude as Jesus. There is no basis for the too-common assumption that Euodia and Syntyche were silly women involved in a petty dispute. Chrysostom did not mention a quarrel or a disagreement and offered only praise: "Do you see how great a testimony [Paul] bears to their virtue?" (Homily 13 on Philippians).

> Greet Mary, who has laboured hard for you ... Greet those labourers in the Lord, Tryphaena and Tryphosa. Greet our dear friend Persis, who has laboured hard in the Lord. Romans 16:6.12 (own translation).

Paul does not indicate what these women were doing other than toiling hard. If 1 Thessalonians 5:12-13 is a guide, however, they may have been involved in leading and caring (*proistēmi*) for their congregations and in advising and instructing fellow believers.[66] We are told that Mary, in particular, worked hard for the members of the church at Rome (Ro 16:6). On the other hand, if Paul's use of 'labour' to describe his apostolic ministry is a guide, perhaps the women were involved in evangelism. Whatever the case, all four women were hard workers involved in significant ministries endorsed by Paul. In 1 Corinthians 16:16, Paul told the Corinthian church to submit to everyone who ministers as a coworker and labourer. Cooperating with such ministers would make their hard work easier.

Andronicus and Junia

Not only was ministry difficult, it could be dangerous. Paul faced dangers many times, as did other Christian ministers. Paul acknowledges, for example, that Prisca and Aquila had risked their necks for him (Ro 16:4).

From the beginning, Christian women and men were persecuted, imprisoned, and even killed for their faith and ministry. Before his Damascus Road experience, Paul himself was responsible for the imprisonment and murder of Christians. He admitted, 'I persecuted the followers of this Way to their death, arresting both men and women and throwing them into prison' (Acts 22:4 NIV; cf. Acts 8:3; 9:1ff). In Romans 16:7, we hear about a missionary couple who were imprisoned with Paul, presumably because of their ministry.

> Greet Andronicus and Junia, my fellow Jews who have been in prison with me. They are outstanding among the apostles, and they were in Christ before I was. Romans 16:7 (NIV)

Andronicus and Junia may have been husband and wife, or brother and sister, but Junia's identity as a woman has been hidden in some texts and

---

[66] It may be that in all eight occurrences of the word *proistēmi* in the New Testament—in Romans 12:8, 1 Thessalonians 5:12, 1 Timothy 3:4.5.12, 5:17, and Titus 3:8.14—there is a sense of caring and providing for combined with a sense of leading or managing.

translations. Some thought she was a man named Junias.⁶⁷ However, the masculine name Junias does not exist in ancient inscriptions or literature, whereas the feminine name is well attested. Furthermore, ancient and medieval commentators on Romans overwhelmingly understood Junia to be a woman.⁶⁸

Others have baulked at the idea that Junia, a woman, was an apostle. Andronicus and Junia were not among the Twelve, but there are people who are called apostles in the New Testament who were not among the Twelve. These other apostles include Paul, Barnabas (Acts 14:3-4.14), Apollos (1 Cor 1:12), anonymous brothers with an important mission (2 Cor 8:23), Silas and Timothy (1 Thess 2:6; cf. 1 Thess 1:1), Epaphroditus (Phil 2:25), as well as Andronicus and Junia.

An apostle (*apostolos*) is someone who is 'sent' (*apostellō*) on a mission. Church history is full of examples of men and women who have been sent by the church or been driven by a personal calling to pioneer ministries that have furthered the gospel, ministries that can be described as apostolic. Chrysostom, a native Greek speaker, understood that Paul had counted Junia as 'worthy of the appellation of apostle' (Homily 31 on Romans).

Andronicus and Junia's apostolic ministry landed them in jail. Perhaps their message had caused a disturbance. Prisons in ancient times were often dark, cramped, putrid, and generally miserable places. Prisoners could be chained or placed in stocks. And women, such as Junia, could be sexually abused by male prison guards. Furthermore, if Andronicus and Junia were freedmen, rather than having the status of freeborn Roman citizens, their imprisonment would most likely have involved torture. Nevertheless, Paul mentions their imprisonment, and states their other credentials, as a way of honouring them as an outstanding missionary couple.

VI. Paul's theology of ministry and I Timothy 2:12

Paul mentions at least eighteen women in his letters and he speaks about them in terms of their faith and ministry. He uses the same ministry terms—coworker, *diakonos*, brother/sister, apostle, and labourer—for both his male and female ministry colleagues, and there is not the slightest

---

67 In a few texts and translations, Euodia (Phil 4:2-3) and Nympha (Col 4:15) have also been turned into men with the masculine names Euodias and Nymphas. But the scholarly consensus is that these individuals, as well as Junia, were women.

68 A list of early and medieval Christian scholars who took the name to be feminine is on my website. https://margmowczko.com/junias-junia-julia-romans-167/.

hint of censure from him about women who functioned as leaders in their churches.[69] Nevertheless, after Paul's time, women were increasingly restricted and were excluded from many of the ministries that were open to their brothers.

People who limit the ministry of women frequently cite 1 Timothy 2:12 to support their position.

> *I do not permit a woman to teach or to domineer*[70] *a man; rather, she is to be quiet. 1 Timothy 2:12 (own translation)*

This verse is not prohibiting the ministry of well-behaved and educated women. This becomes apparent when we pull back from this one verse and look at its immediate context, the context of problem behaviour.

In 1 Timothy 2:8, Paul addresses the problem of angry, quarrelling men in the Ephesian church; 'men' is plural. In 1 Timothy 2:9-10, Paul addresses the problem of overdressed rich Ephesian women; 'women' is plural. Then in verses 11-15, Paul addresses the problem of a woman who needed to learn and was not allowed to teach. Presumably, she needed to learn scripture and Christian doctrine. She was also not allowed to domineer a man, probably her husband. 'Woman' and 'man' are singular in verses 11-12. There is also a singular verb in verse 15 correctly translated as 'she will be saved': she will be saved if they (the married couple) continue in faith, love and holiness. I suggest 1 Timothy 2:11-15 is about a couple in the Ephesian church, and that the wife was teaching and behaving badly.

In 1 Timothy 2:13-14 Paul gives correct summary statements of Genesis 2 and 3. It is not clear why he mentions Adam and Eve, but it may have been to correct the woman's faulty teaching of the Law (Torah), perhaps a corrupted version of Genesis 2 and 3 that favoured Eve (cf. 1 Tim 1:3-4.7). There were allegorical, fanciful, and distorted versions of the Adam and Eve story circulating in the first century.

1 Timothy 2:15 is a difficult verse to decipher but it may be about the woman's domineering behaviour towards her husband. She may have been refusing sex and avoiding childbirth for reasons of piety. Some in the Ephesian church were even forbidding marriage (1 Tim 4:3a). Sexual renun-

---

[69] Paul does not refer to any of his ministry colleagues as bishops (*episkopoi*), elders/presbyters, or pastors. Though he uses these terms a few times in his letters, he does not identify or describe any individual with these terms.

[70] The Greek word behind "to domineer" is *authentein*. This word does not refer to a healthy kind of authority, but to a controlling and absolute use of power that is unacceptable from men or women. More information on *authentein* is available on my website: https://margmowczko.com/tag/authentein/.

ciation was not uncommon in the early church. Much of 1 Corinthians 7 was written in response to the issue of married and single Corinthian Christians who were choosing to become and remain celibate.

In 1 Timothy 2:8-15, Paul addresses problem behaviour of specific men and specific women in the Ephesian church and he offers corrections. Paul also gave directives about problem behaviour of both men and women in 1 Corinthians 14:26-40. This passage contains the verses 1 Corinthians 14:34-35: 'women are to be silent in the churches . . .' These passages in 1 Timothy and 1 Corinthians, about issues in the Ephesian and Corinthian churches, are not Paul's general thoughts about ministry. The apostle's overall theology of ministry was, 'You have a gift, use it to build up the church,' and he does not exclude women from his general statements about ministry, including leadership and teaching ministries, in Romans 12:6-8, 1 Corinthians chapter 12, and Ephesians 4:11-13.

Conclusion

Paul valued women and endorsed their ministries. He planted a church in Lydia's home. He introduced Phoebe to the church at Rome as his sister, as a minister or deacon, as a patron of many (including himself), and he entrusted his letter to the Romans to her. He valued the ministries of Prisca, Euodia, and Syntyche as his coworkers in the gospel. He positively acknowledged the ministry labours of Mary of Rome, Tryphena, Tryphosa, and Persis. He referred to Junia as a fellow Jew, his fellow prisoner, and as outstanding among the apostles. Paul warmly mentions no less than ten women in Romans chapter 16.

There are still more women who Paul acknowledges in his letters. He took seriously a report from Chloe of Corinth's people. He passed on greetings from Claudia of Rome and sent greetings to Apphia of Colossae. He recognized the house church of Nympha in Laodicea and asked that greetings be passed on to her and her church.[71] He respected the faith and teaching of Lois and Eunice.

If the example of these women was the starting point and focus in discussions on women in ministry, I suspect the church and the world would be in a better state. The church benefits when the gifts, talents, perspectives, and life experiences of both men and women are used without artificial restrictions. The church is stronger when men and women can minister together and work side by side.

---

[71] See my article, *Nympha: A House Church Leader in the Lycus Valley*. https://margmowczko.com/nympha-house-church-colossians-415/

The New Testament shows that in the first century, just as today, there were different ways of organizing ministries. Some churches were mostly led by men, others were led by women or by women and men together. But nowhere in the New Testament are godly and capable women expressly forbidden from ministering in any particular capacity.

How would it change our churches if we acknowledge that the apostle Paul valued and endorsed the ministries of gifted women and did not limit them? Who are the women in your church that God wants to use as ministers and leaders?

Reflection Questions

1. What is your understanding of the Bible's teaching on women ministers? Have any ideas in this chapter challenged that view or supported it?

2. Does it correspond or conflict with the examples of Phoebe and Priscilla? And how would you explain your view to young men and women in your context?

Lessons from History: how Culture can Distort Interpretation of Scripture

Andrew Bartlett

I. Starting with the Bible

There are many indications in the Bible that God values women and men equally and commissions both women and men as his image-bearers and representatives in the world (for example, Gen 1:27-28; Acts 2:17-18; 1 Cor 12:4-11; Gal 3:26-29).

In ancient Israel men's and women's responsibilities overlapped. To provide and protect was not the exclusive responsibility of men. As opportunity arose, women also served their families and communities by providing and protecting.[72] They even founded new settlements or towns (1 Chron 7:24). While most leaders were men, there was no rule which debarred women from leadership or from public life. They served in leading the nation, including as prophets.[73]

The only task formally prohibited to women was to serve in the Levitical priesthood, for this was reserved to a restricted group of able-bodied men from one family. This foreshadowed the unique function of Jesus the Messiah, who himself replaced the Levitical priesthood, and who inaugurated a universal 'priesthood' of all those who believe in him, both men and women (Heb 2-10; 1 Pet 2:9; Rev 1:6; 5:10).[74]

In the New Testament, Jesus welcomes women as his disciples, appears first to women at his resurrection, and pours the Holy Spirit on women as on men. In the young churches, women are co-workers, prophets and patrons, hosting assemblies of believers in their houses; Junia is an apostle, working in partnership with Andronicus.[75] Women who follow Jesus Christ are persecuted and imprisoned, alongside men (Acts 8:3; Rom 16:7).

---

[72] Andrew Bartlett, *Men and Women in Christ: Fresh Light from the Biblical Texts* (London: IVP, 2019), 86-89. I will refer to this book as *Men and Women in Christ*. This present chapter re-uses some material from the book.

[73] For discussion of Miriam, Huldah, Deborah, and the unnamed wise woman of 2 Samuel 20, see *Men and Women in Christ*, 91-95.

[74] *Men and Women in Christ*, 291-292.

[75] *Men and Women in Christ*, 8-9, 295-312. Also Acts 2:33. On the significance of Jesus' initial choice of 12 male apostles, see *Men and Women in Christ*, 289-291.

While the Bible is clear that men and women stand in the same relation to God, and receive spiritual gifts without gender distinction, history shows that human beings do not consistently live in a manner that is true to this understanding. Human sinfulness gets in the way. And human culture has a way of distorting how we read and interpret the Bible.

II. The example of Calvin

In sixteenth-century Europe, it was widely regarded as unacceptable that women might be called by God to teach and lead both men and women. John Calvin (1509-1564), a highly gifted teacher of the Bible, lived in this culture. In his *Commentary on 1 Timothy* he interpreted 1 Timothy 2:12 to mean that Paul excluded all women in the church 'from the office of teaching, which God has committed to men only.'

But Calvin was a keen student of the Bible. So he was aware that there were obvious scriptural objections to this interpretation. It appeared inconsistent with the story of Deborah in Judges 4-5: did not that story show that God may call women to lead and instruct both women and men? His interpretation also appeared inconsistent with the evidence of women prophets and teachers in the New Testament, where the Lord distributed spiritual gifts without gender distinction (Rom 12:1-8; 1 Cor 12:1-11; Eph 4:6-13). What about Priscilla teaching Apollos (Acts 18:26), or Junia serving as an apostle (Rom 16:7), or Philip's daughters prophesying (Acts 21:9)?

How did Calvin deal with those objections? He wrote:

> If any one bring forward, by way of objection, Deborah (Judges 4:4) and others of the same class, of whom we read that they were at one time appointed by the command of God to govern the people, the answer is easy. Extraordinary acts done by God do not overturn the ordinary rules of government, by which he intended that we should be bound. Accordingly, if women at one time held the office of prophets and teachers, and that too when they were supernaturally called to it by the Spirit of God, He who is above all law might do this; but, being a peculiar case, this is not opposed to the constant and ordinary system of government.

He went on to explain that government by women–

> ... has always been regarded by all wise persons as a monstrous thing.

This provides a vivid example of how the tide of culture can carry a person's thoughts off track, so as to silence what Scripture is saying. Calvin admits that he sees in Scripture that God commanded Deborah to govern

Lessons from History: how Culture can Distort Interpretation of Scripture

the nation. He is aware of women prophets in both Testaments. He knows the story of Priscilla, for in his *Commentary on Acts* he acknowledges that in Acts 18:26 'we see that one of the chief teachers of the Church was instructed by a woman'. And he has a good understanding of Junia's ministry, explaining in his *Commentary on Romans* that she was not one of the Twelve but an apostle in the sense of 'those who not only teach in one Church, but also spend their labour in promulgating the gospel everywhere' and planting churches. He therefore knows that the sovereign God distributes gifts of teaching and leadership as he wills, including to women.

But Calvin cannot bring himself to accept the significance of what he sees. His appeal to the fact that God does extraordinary acts does not satisfactorily resolve the dissonance between Scripture and Calvin's own teaching. He portrays God as commanding something monstrous (namely, that a woman, Deborah, should govern) and as being unwise (since *all wise persons* have *always* regarded government by women as a monstrous thing). This is dishonouring to God. Why does Calvin not perceive that this is so? It is the effect of the culture in which he swims.

In a similar way, cultural understanding determines Calvin's reading of the next verse, 1 Timothy 2:13. He is candid about his own puzzlement over how Paul's reference to Adam being created 'first' supports a universal rule of women's subordination under male leaders. As he says:

> ... the reason Paul assigns, that woman was second in order of creation, appears not to be a very strong argument in favour of her subjection; for John the Baptist was before Christ in the order of time, and yet was greatly inferior in rank.

But a cultural overlay to the Genesis story provides an answer that he feels is satisfactory:

> ... the woman was created afterwards, in order that she might be a kind of appendage to the man; and ... she was joined to the man on the express condition, that she should be at hand to render obedience to him (Genesis 2:21).

It does not matter to Calvin that Genesis 2 does not in fact present the woman as a kind of appendage to the man, but instead as a powerful ally, equal and complementary to the man. Nor does it matter to him that Genesis 2 says not a single word about woman's duty to render obedience to man. He is not deterred even by the fact that John Chrysostom, whom Calvin quotes in his commentaries more than any other author, expressly acknowledges that there is nothing in Genesis 2 about women's obedience to men.[76] Doubtless, in Calvin's culture the correct understanding seemed to him to be obvious. He therefore imagines Paul reading Genesis 2 in line with his own cultural understanding, despite the lack of any explicit justification for this in the biblical text.[77]

John Calvin was one of the greatest teachers of the Church. His commentaries are still read today with great profit, nearly 500 years after they were written. He was a man of deep learning, who sincerely sought to expound the Bible faithfully. He therefore serves as an outstanding example of the sometimes overwhelming impact of culture on interpretation of Scripture.

III. The traditional majority view

Seen in historical perspective, Calvin's sixteenth-century European view of women was not particularly distinctive. His claim, that all wise persons have always regarded government by women as a monstrous thing, reminds us that he was not relying simply on the particular culture in which he lived, but on a view of women that had been widely shared across different cultures over many centuries. In his *Commentary on 1 Corinthians* he wrote (in reference to 14:34):

> Unquestionably, wherever even natural propriety has been maintained, women have in all ages been excluded from the public management of affairs. It is the dictate of common sense, that female government is improper and unseemly.

It may be striking to us that in his exposition he appeals to 'natural propriety' and 'common sense' rather than to Scripture. But he could have cited many Christian teachers from earlier times whose idea of propriety and common sense regarding women was similar to his own. From about the late second century onwards, we find a traditional majority view among Christian teachers that women were inferior to men, both in rank and in nature. Compared with men, women were understood to be inherently

---

[76] Chrysostom, *1 Corinthians*, Homily 26: 'she was not subjected as soon as she was made; nor, when He brought her to the man, did either she hear any such thing from God, nor did the man say any such word to her: ... of rule or subjection he no where made mention unto her.' For more on Genesis 2 and its presentation of woman as man's powerful ally, see *Men and Women in Christ* chapter 5. For Calvin's view of Chrysostom, see *Men and Women in Christ*, 299.

[77] For a full discussion of 1 Timothy 2, see *Men and Women in Christ*, chapters 11-13 and appendices 3-6.

defective, being less intelligent, more prone to sin, unfit for the kinds of leadership that men could provide, and not in God's image in the same full sense as men. And aspects of this vein of teaching continued long after Calvin's time and even into the twenty-first century.

Here are some examples from across the centuries:

Clement of Alexandria (about 190):

> The mark of the man, the beard, by which he is seen to be a man, is older than Eve, and is the token of the superior nature.
>
> *(The Instructor 3.3)*

Augustine of Hippo (about 418):

> The woman together with her own husband is the image of God, so that that whole substance may be one image; but when she is referred separately to her quality of help-meet, which regards the woman herself alone, then she is not the image of God; but as regards the man alone, he is the image of God as fully and completely as when the woman is joined with him in one.
>
> *(The Trinity 12.7)*

> That a man endowed with a spiritual mind could have believed this [the lie of the serpent] is astonishing. And just because it is impossible to believe it, woman was given to man, woman who was of small intelligence and who perhaps still lives more in accordance with the promptings of the inferior flesh than by the superior reason.
>
> *(Literal Commentary on Genesis 11:42)*

Albertus Magnus (about 1258):

> For a woman is a flawed male and, in comparison to the male, has the nature of defect and privation, and this is why naturally she mistrusts herself. And this is why whatever she cannot acquire on her own she strives to acquire through mendacity and diabolical deceptions. Therefore, to speak briefly, one must be as mistrustful of every woman as of a venomous serpent and a horned devil ... the female is more prudent, that is, cleverer, than the male with respect to evil and perverse deeds ... In this way, the woman falls short in intellectual operations, which consist in the apprehension of the good and in knowledge of truth and flight from evil ... sense moves the female to every evil, just as intellect moves a man to every good.
>
> *(Questions concerning Aristotle's On Animals, Book 15, Question 11: Whether the male is better suited for proper behaviour [mores] than the female)*

Thomas Aquinas (1273):

> As regards the individual nature, woman is defective and misbegotten ...
> *(Summa Theologica, Question 92, Article 1, Reply to Objection 1)*

> Woman is naturally subject to man, because in man the discretion of reason predominates.
> *(Summa Theologica, Question 92, Article 1, Reply to Objection 2)*

Martin Luther (1535):

> The woman, although she was a most beautiful work of God, nevertheless was not the equal of the male in glory and prestige ... this sex ... is inferior to the male sex.
> *(Lectures on Genesis 1 – 5, Gen 1:27)*

John Knox (1558):

> Who can deny but it is repugnant to nature, that the blind shall be appointed to lead and conduct such as do see? And ... that the foolish, mad, and frenetic shall govern the discreet, and give counsel to such as be sober of mind? And such be all women, compared unto man in bearing of authority. For their sight in civil regiment [*government*] is but blindness; their strength, weakness; their counsel, foolishness; and judgment, frenzy, if it be rightly considered.
> *(First Blast of the Trumpet against the Monstrous Regiment of Women)*

Richard Hooker (1597):

> [T]hings equal in every respect are never willingly directed one by another: woman therefore was even in her first estate framed by Nature, not only after in time, but inferior in excellency also unto man ... [I]n ancient times ... women ... were in marriage delivered unto their husbands by others. Which custom retained hath still this use, that it putteth women in mind of a duty whereunto the very imbecility of their nature and sex doth bind them; namely to be always directed, guided and ordered by others.
> *(Of the Laws of Ecclesiastical Polity 5.73)*

Adam Clarke (about 1831):

> The structure of woman's body plainly proves that she was never designed for those exertions required in public life. In this the chief part of the natural inferiority of woman is to be sought.
> *(The Holy Bible with a Commentary and Critical Notes, 1 Tim 2:13)*

Charles Hodge (1860):

> The ground of the obligation [of wife's obedience] ... is the eminency of the husband; his superiority in those attributes which enable and entitle him to command ... This superiority of the man ... thus taught in Scripture, founded in nature, and proved by all experience, cannot be denied ...
> *(A Commentary on the Epistle to the Ephesians, Eph 5:23)*

Douglas Moo (1980):

> Paul cites Eve's failure as exemplary and perhaps causative of the nature of women in general and ... this susceptibility to deception bars them from engaging in public teaching.
> *(I Timothy 2:11-15: Meaning and Significance)*

Mark Driscoll (2004):

> ... when it comes to leading in the church, women are unfit because they are more gullible and easier to deceive than men. While many irate women have disagreed with his [Paul's] assessment through the years, it does appear from this that such women who fail to trust his instruction and follow his teaching are much like their mother Eve and are well-intentioned but ill-informed ...
> *(Church Leadership: Explaining the Roles of Jesus, Elders, Deacons, and Members at Mars Hill)*[78]

---

[78] Extract from Augustine's Literal Commentary on Genesis is quoted by Elizabeth A. Clark, *Women in the Early Church*. Message of the Fathers of the Church 13 (Wilmington: Michael Glazier, 1983), 40. Extract from Albertus Magnus is from Irven M. Resnick and Kenneth F. Kitchell, Jr, trans. *Albert the Great: Questions Concerning Aristotle's On Animals*. Vol. 9 of *The Fathers of the Church: Mediaeval Continuation* (Washington DC: Catholic University of America Press, 2008), 454. Extract from Luther is from Jaroslav Pelikan, ed. *Luther's Works*, Vol. 1: *Lectures on Genesis: Chapters 1-5* (St Louis: Concordia, 1958), 69. Extract from Moo is *Trinity Journal 1 NS* (1980): 62-83, 70. He partly changed his mind at *Trinity Journal 2 NS* (1981): 198-222, 204 ('the difficulties with viewing v 14 as a statement about the nature of women are real'). Extract from Driscoll is from Mars Hill Theology Series (Seattle: Mars Hill Church, 2004), cited at https://www.dennyburk.com/a-mere-complementarian-reading-of-the-most-contested-verse-in-the-evangelical-gender-debate-1-timothy-212/ posted 23 January 2018. Other extracts are from published versions in the public domain and available online.

IV. Other views and other realities

Despite these many expressions of opinion by well-known Christian teachers and leaders, we should not imagine that the traditional majority view of women's inferiority and incompetence was universally or consistently held by Christians up to recent times. The New Testament view of men's and women's equality, and of the competence of gifted women to teach and lead, has had defenders throughout church history. Moreover, many have adhered to the New Testament vision in part, even though not in full.

To see the true distinctiveness of the New Testament's vision of women, we need to have an accurate understanding of women's place in first-century cultures. We should not assume that women were always excluded from leadership and authority. In New Testament times leadership by women, whether of local organizations, of provinces, or even of empires, was far from unknown. To name a few examples approximately contemporary with Paul:

- In Pompeii, Eumachia was a public figure, as priestess of Venus and possibly patroness of the fullers' guild. Other women were also patronesses of guilds.
- King Agrippa shared power with his sister, Bernice (Acts 25:13).
- The Kandake was the female ruler of the Ethiopians (Acts 8:27).
- When the youthful Nero first became emperor of Rome, it was his mother, Agrippina, who was in charge, as is shown by the way in which they were depicted together on Roman coinage.
- In remote eastern Britain, Boudicca was a queen and war leader.[79]

In what way was the Christian view of women, as found in the New Testament, truly different? The New Testament showed that *all* women, not merely the few powerful exceptions who became leaders, should be treated with respect, as full persons, equal to men. From the early days, Christian believers came to understand that in God's sight women were of equal worth with men, and that they were equally recipients of God's grace and promises. Over time this was a major factor in the growth of the gospel across the Greek and Roman world.[80]

---

[79] For further information, see *Men and Women in Christ*, 311.
[80] Rodney Stark, *The Rise of Christianity: How the Obscure, Marginal Jesus Movement Became the Dominant Religious Force in the Western World in a Few Centuries* (Princeton: Princeton University Press, 1996), 95-128.

Some early Christian writings, before traditional patriarchalism largely recaptured the Christian imagination, reflect the biblical perspective of an equal partnership of men and women. Around the year 200, Tertullian wrote these words about Christian marriage, inspired by 1 Corinthians 7:39 and other scriptures:

> What kind of yoke is that of two believers, of one hope, one desire, one discipline, one and the same service? Both brethren, both fellow servants, no difference of spirit or of flesh; nay, truly 'two in one flesh'. Where the flesh is one, one is the spirit too. Together they pray, together prostrate themselves, together perform their fasts; mutually teaching, mutually exhorting, mutually sustaining ... Between the two echo psalms and hymns; and they mutually challenge each other which shall better chant to their Lord ... These are the things which that utterance of the apostle has, beneath its brevity, left to be understood by us.[81]

Similarly, John Chrysostom (late fourth century): although he mostly regarded the women of his own day as incompetent, he clearly taught that in New Testament times women were preachers and teachers of the word in partnership with men, including the apostle Junia, who worked in partnership with Andronicus.[82]

In church history there are many examples of gifted Christian women who were able to teach and lead in a variety of ways. In the fourth century, Marcella and Paula worked closely with Jerome. In the twelfth century, the abbess Hildegard of Bingen advised emperors, popes and bishops. In the sixteenth, Argula von Stauffer was a staunch defender of Luther; and Katherine Zell ministered with her husband Matthew and alone after his death. In the seventeenth, Anne Hutchinson led both men and women in New England. In the eighteenth, Mary Fletcher was a powerful preacher in the Methodist movement. In the nineteenth, Phoebe Palmer was a Methodist

---

[81] Tertullian, *To His Wife* 2.8. The 'utterance of the apostle' is 1 Cor 7:39 – marriage 'in the Lord' (see *To His Wife* 2.1), expounded with allusions to Eph 4:4; 1 Cor 12:5; Gal 3:28; Eph 5:31; Col 3:16. Tertullian was not always consistent; on other occasions he wrote negatively about women.

[82] In Homily 73 on Matthew 23:14 he contrasts the women of his own day with New Testament women who, without bringing evil report upon themselves, 'went about with the apostles, having taken unto themselves manly courage, Priscilla, Persis, and the rest; ... even travelling into far countries ... [T]he business of those women was to spread the word.' Regarding Andronicus and Junia, see his Homily 31 on Romans, further discussed in *Men and Women in Christ*, 299-306.

holiness leader; and Catherine Booth was an effective preacher in the Salvation Army, alongside her husband William.[83]

Notably, in the late nineteenth and early twentieth century conservative evangelicals were more open to women's leadership and ministry than they later became.[84] This openness was reversed part way through the twentieth century.

Why the reverse? It appears that there was an over-reaction to cultural changes in wider society, especially in the United States of America. Fears about feminization, radical feminism, godless socialism, and other perceived threats provoked not merely a justified resistance to unbiblical ideas but also a strong movement in reaction. This movement replaced the Jesus of the New Testament with a false icon of dominant masculinity. Evangelical Christian belief became associated in the minds of many with rugged male dominance and nationalistic military prowess.[85] I recently attended a Men's Convention where the speaker, a pastor with a prominent role on behalf of the Council of Biblical Manhood and Womanhood, presented Jesus as an icon of powerful masculinity. He urged that Christian men should work at being truly 'masculine', exercising dominion over women. To inspire us to greater masculinity, he told a story which conjured a stirring Hollywood image of the macho alpha male, who does not hesitate to use violence to resolve a situation. This seems a far cry from the New Testament, where both men and women are equally called to be truly

---

[83] For more information about these women and others, see Ronald W. Pierce, and Rebecca Merrill Groothuis, eds., *Discovering Biblical Equality: Complementarity without Hierarchy*, 2nd ed. (Downers Grove: InterVarsity Press, 2005), chapters 1 and 2.

[84] See Timothy Larsen, 'Women in Public Ministry: A Historic Evangelical Distinctive.' In *Women, Ministry and the Gospel: Exploring New Paradigms*, ed. Mark Husbands and Timothy Larsen (Downers Grove: InterVarsity Press, 2007), 213–236. A shorter version of Larsen's excellent essay is available at https://perspectivesjournal.org/posts/evangelicalisms-strong-history-women-ministry/.

[85] See Kristin Kobes Du Mez, *Jesus and John Wayne: How White Evangelicals Corrupted a Faith and Fractured a Nation* (New York: Norton, 2020). In 2014 Dr Owen Strachan, Senior Fellow and former President of the Council on Biblical Manhood and Womanhood tweeted an unorthodox new insight into what happened at the Cross: 'Satan hates testosterone. You can't blame him—after all, he's seen it used to crush his head.' https://twitter.com/ostrachan/status/499933939767574529?lang=en (accessed 12 September 2020). Because of the culture of which he is part, in which Christlikeness is seen in terms of muscular masculine dominance (in contrast to the New Testament, where to be like Christ is the goal for both men and women) it doubtless seemed to Dr Strachan to be quite unexceptionable to say that it was a male sex hormone which won our Lord's victory on the Cross.

Christ-like, serving in humility and never repaying evil with evil (Mt 5:5.38-48; Mk 10:42-45; Rom 8:29, 12:14-21; 1 Cor 11:1; 2 Cor 5:17; Gal 3:26-28; 5:13-14; Eph 5:2; 1 Pet 3:9; 1 Jn 3:2). Nonetheless, despite this powerful cultural movement within evangelicalism, survey evidence suggests that even in the United States a large majority of evangelicals support women preachers, including at a church's main Sunday morning gathering.[86]

V. Minimizing our cultural distortions

To twenty-first century readers, interpretive moves which evade the teaching of the Bible by appealing to what 'all wise persons' are said to think, or to a standard of 'common sense' which we no longer share, appear obviously questionable. But they are a warning to us, since every age and every culture has its own blind spots. What can we do to guard against this fact of life?

In *Men and Women in Christ: Fresh Light from the Biblical Texts*, I describe an interpretation toolbox of seven tools which can help Bible readers to adopt a position of appropriate humility before the text, where we open ourselves to what the Bible teaches and allow it to challenge our preconceived ideas. Space permits only a brief discussion of them here.[87]

1. Primacy of Scripture over tradition

Tradition is entitled to respect. It is instructive to read Scripture with those who wore different cultural spectacles from our own. We do not lightly set aside traditions and interpretations held by Christians in former days, who have prayed and worshipped and served God, and have sought to be faithful in interpreting the Bible. But, if the Bible is in conflict with tradition, the words of Scripture must prevail. (This is the central reason

---

[86] According to research published in *Christianity Today*, 72.8% of US evangelicals believe women should be allowed to preach at church on Sunday morning and 82.1% believe they should be allowed to lead worship: https://www.christianitytoday.com/ct/2020/june-web-only/research-evangelicals-women-leaders-complementarian-preach.html published 30 June 2020. In the US context the term 'evangelical' has a wide range of meaning, and is often understood to have as much political as theological content. However, this finding is in line with earlier evidence (cited in the same article) that as at 2011 65% of Southern Baptists were supportive of women being allowed to serve as pastors, even though since 2000 the official position of the Southern Baptist Convention has been that this is prohibited.

[87] See the fuller discussion in *Men and Women in Christ*, appendix 1, 359-367.

for today's disagreement with the long-standing custom of placing restrictions on women's ministry; those restrictions are not faithful to Scripture.)

2. Paying appropriate positive attention to culture

Biblical writers were not modern Western thinkers. We must enter into their thought-world in order to gain an accurate understanding of their meaning.

The doctrine of the 'clarity' or 'perspicuity' of Scripture means that Scripture is clear enough for us to know what God requires and his offer of salvation. It does not mean that everything is clear to every subsequent reader, or that the whole of Scripture can be accurately understood without any background knowledge of the cultural world of the writers and the first readers. Awareness of background enables us to avoid or minimize distortions derived from our own culture and worldviews.

3. Going back to the source language in context

Translations are affected by translators' own traditions and cultures and also by their understanding of the source culture. The impacts of culture and of translation traditions are particularly powerful upon verses bearing on gender relations, and therefore require special attention to guard against them. The process of making corrections to passages affected by cultural bias against women is still under way.[88] We therefore need to go back to the source language in its context.

Where there is uncertainty over meaning, we must pay appropriate attention to how the same words are used elsewhere. But it is not enough to study individual words, because the way they are used in other contexts only provides possible meanings; the actual meaning must depend upon the particular context.

Caution is also needed because the important question is not 'what do the individual words mean?' It is 'what did the author intend to convey?'[89] When considering context, we have to take into account the literary

---

[88] See further appendix 7 of *Men and Women in Christ*, where many passages affected in this way are identified.

[89] It follows from belief in God's inspiration of Scripture that an early scripture may sometimes be seen, in the light of later scriptures, to have a fuller significance of which the original author may have been unaware. But this possibility does not bear significantly on the present topic.

context (the surrounding words) and the historical context (the situation on the ground, in so far as we can determine it), as well as the wider cultural context. Words are elastic. To determine meaning, context is always king.

4. Coherence

We should do the biblical writers the honour of attending very closely to what they write, so as to discover their actual reasoning and message. Therefore, within any particular passage of Scripture, we should seek a coherent and internally consistent interpretation which accurately accounts for everything said in the passage.

5. A Christ-centred canonical approach

The Bible is God's story with the world, a story about the coming of the Messiah. The Lord Jesus Christ must therefore be central to our understanding. He is the Word of God. The written word must be understood in the light of him. He is the one that we follow.

The canonical approach is an aspect of using context wisely. The Holy Spirit who inspired the scriptures does not contradict himself. But to understand correctly we must keep in mind the progression of the Messiah's story and where we fit into it. We are living after the resurrection of Jesus Christ and the gift of the Holy Spirit at Pentecost, and we look forward to the grand finale that is to come. God's word is given to us so that we may live out our part in God's great story.

6. Spiritual openness

Paul tells us that, for understanding God's purposes, natural abilities are not sufficient. We need discernment given by God's Spirit (1 Cor 2:9-16). For Christian leaders who have become committed to a particular viewpoint, it is an immensely challenging task to look at a topic again with fresh eyes and an open mind, even if they do so with the utmost effort and prayerfulness.

There can be deep emotional obstacles to open listening, not least in the debates about men and women. We need to acknowledge the strong feelings that arise in these debates, so that we can be realistic about how our feelings may influence our understanding.

Above all, we need to keep coming back to the text of the Bible with humility, recognizing that we always have more to learn.

7. Practical wisdom

Appreciation of someone else's point of view is made much more difficult when they deploy weak arguments. But we need to be on the alert when what is served up for consideration is unpersuasive. The fact that someone presents poor arguments does not show that they are in the wrong. Their position may be justified by good reasons which they have not thought of, or which have become obscured among the dross. In the same way, when wrestling with the interpretation of Scripture we must not let the weakness of scholars' poorer arguments distract us from seeing the strength of their better ones.

It is also wise to read and listen to a wide range of points of view, since this can both drive us to re-examine our assumptions and provide perspectives that we would otherwise have missed.

VI. Reflection Questions

1. In what ways and to what extent was Jesus' behaviour towards women in conflict with traditional views? Can you give examples?

2. What are your thoughts on the seven tools in the interpretation toolbox? Do you agree or disagree with them? Would you explain them differently? Are other tools needed in order to guard against cultural distortions when interpreting Scripture?

3. This chapter mentions some women leaders from across church history. To what extent are their names and stories familiar to you? Are there Christian women leaders in the history of the church in your own country?

Stories Today

The first section of the book set out to look afresh at biblical perspectives on men and women working effectively together: rather than tip-toe round some theological minefields, we sought to examine them with gracious honesty.

In this second section, we focus on the living out of one's theology. We compiled stories of personal experience to give insights on how we can honour our co-workers. All the writers want to see healthy male and female partnership in the Church and in family life.

Aged from their thirties to fifties, the story-tellers come from a mix of cultures and all of them remind us that the Holy Spirit looks at the heart when gifting men and women. There is something that we all can learn from their pain, humour and hard-won wisdom.

Enjoy dipping into these stories, which are introduced by Rev Gabriel and Rev Jeanette Salguero from the United States.

For your reflection, you will find some questions at the end of all the stories in the section "The Journey of Learning".

Partnership Intended by God

Reverends Gabriel & Jeanette Salguero

> *Two are better than one; because they have a good reward for their labor. For if they fall, the one will lift up his fellow (Ecc 4:9-10, KJV).*

The words of *Qohelet* – the Preacher – are instructive when speaking of work and ministry. Ecclesiastes reminds us that the toil of any vocation, if pursued with the wrong ambition, can often lead to exhaustion and a sense of nihilism. Certainly, the admonishment against vanity and meaninglessness is a necessary caution in our generation where the twin temptations of narcissism and isolation often seduce many leaders in congregations, denominations, and networks to "go-it alone" and can produce burnout. The wise counsel of *Qohelet* begins with this cautionary phrase, "There is one alone, and there is not a second" (Ecc 4:8, KJV)." In this work, you will read the echoes of *Qohelet* to our generation, in the words of the *Rise in Strength Declaration*, "We call on men and women of the global Church to act so that women, men, girls and boys can all embrace their spiritual giftings to strengthen the work of the Church, and Her witness to the glory of God." Partnership and collaboration are at the heart of a Triune God who is in eternal relationship and collaboration in the Godhead.

Partnership empowers

While partnership may be challenging, it is also deeply empowering. This model of leadership, like leadership in general, requires us to navigate our egos and pride in ways that ensure both respect and Kingdom advancement. Ministry collaboration deepens our sense of interdependence, humility, and mutuality. For over 15 years, we have worked together as co-founders of the National Latino Evangelical Coalition and as co-lead pastors of several congregations. As co-pastors of The Gathering Place in Orlando, Florida, we have also been deeply and personally enriched by partnerships that highlight the giftings of the people of God in our local congregation. Our story is not unique; there is a renewal movement afoot. God is raising up men and women who understand that the partnership displayed in Creation, marred by the Fall, modeled by Christ, and empowered by the Spirit, is being activated in ministries across the globe. In our travels, we have been inspired to see how many men and women, local church leaders, college students, married and single, are flourishing with a partnership model that is renewing the Church and transforming the world.

To be clear, while we believe no one should work alone, we do not believe that every ministry needs to follow our particular model of co-leadership. God uses many types of leadership models to expand his kingdom. Nevertheless, amid the reticence against partnership in some quarters of global Evangelicalism, we are honored to join the World Evangelical Alliance Women's Commission chorus of voices who remind us the gift that collaboration is to the healthy expansion of the Kingdom of God. We cannot count the number of times Jeanette has been rendered invisible because of the myopic vision around leadership in the modern world. Once we were even asked if Jeanette was the secretary of the project she was leading. Our impaired vision limits our reach. Similarly, the comments around Gabriel's fragility or weakness as a man abounded because we shared leadership. Still, we did not relent because the countless testimonies of Gen-Z and Millennial leaders who embraced a Gospel vision of shared leadership inspired us anew.

Partnership rooted in Scripture

The vision of partnership in leadership and service is not, as some may argue, a new phenomenon but rather a leadership model deeply rooted in the teachings of Scripture, the ministry of Jesus, the empowerment of the Holy Spirit, and exemplars throughout Christian tradition. Much of the opposition to shared leadership is rooted in the faulty assumption that it is a passing post-modern fad rooted in the secular progressive myth. Partnership in ministry is NOT a human project. It is a God-initiative that brings God glory, enhances our Gospel-witness in a pluralistic world, and heals the nations of the earth. Boys and girls from every continent are clamoring for models that empower them to live-out the fullness of their God-given charisms and talents. The time has come to equip this generation of believers with Gospel-centered partnerships centered on humility and service.

In the Gospels, Jesus continuously underlines the power of partnership. From prayer to outreach, Jesus in Matthew 18, teaches the power of agreement when petitioning God in prayer. ". . . if two of you shall agree on earth as touching anything that they shall ask, it shall be done for them (Matt 18:19, KJV)." And again, in Luke, when Christ commissions the seventy disciples in the early days of his earthly ministry he underscores the power of partnership, "and he sent them two by two before his face into every city and place, whither he himself would come (Luke 10:1, KJV)." Jesus lays the foundation of what the Church has too often forgotten, ministry in healthy collaboration yields great and abundant fruit.

Partnership requires work

If we are honest, the call to partnership is often romanticized. The challenges to this model are real. The giants of exploitation, abuse of power, and a hyper-sexualized culture are prevalent and must be conquered. While partnerships can increase Gospel fruitfulness, our propensity to "lord it over one another" looms large. In short, our humanity lurks. For years, we have had to bring together our roles as co-pastors and organizational leaders. Clear communication and mutual submission are in high demand and low supply. It takes great strength to recognize our limitations and others' strengths. Kingdom-collaboration calls us to embrace both the gifts of limitations and the power of synergy. When we celebrate God's gifts to both men and women, we simultaneously embrace the gift of limitations. None of us is all-gifted and our limitations allow us to claim interdependence and celebrate the gifts of our partners. Thank God we do not have to do it all!

The tough work of negotiation is where we have seen the most tension. Hubris is seductive. If the goal of leading is to claim credit or be the headliner, then partnership is not for you. It is precisely the sin of pride that has buried many ministry partnerships. Hubris is subtle because it often masks itself as a sense of competency or pursuit of excellence. Many times, these pretexts are really a claim that no one can do it the way we do it. Jesus reminds us that among us it should not be so (Matt 20:25-26, KJV). The cause of the Gospel ought always to be greater than any selfish ambition or thirst for fame. In our case, this has sparked many a passionate conversation about who is best suited to exercise leadership in a certain area.

Yes, that's correct, passionate conversation is a euphemism for learning the way of surrender. Surrender is a term not commonly associated with leadership, but it is the way of cruciform leadership. The mindfulness required to say, "She or he is better suited to lead in this area," is not weakness but strength. For too long our definition of leadership has been limited to the dimensions of power, giftings and charisma. As we move forward to a Biblical view of partnership, we are reminded that surrender, service and mutuality are deep dimensions of cruciform leadership.

As you read about the models of partnership, both Biblical and contemporary, contained in this book, it is our sincere prayer that God will inspire and raise a generation of men and women committed to honoring God, serving the church, and healing their world with kingdom collaboration.

Impact: Partnership in God between Husband and Wife

Florence Muindi

In the summer of 1995, Festus and I packed up our home in Kenya and stepped out to serve the poor and vulnerable in their nations. We departed with our two sons, a 5 year old and a 6 month old baby, and together as a family entered a journey of faith. Today we testify to the answered prayer of Jesus, *Just as you, Father, are in me and I in you, so they might be one heart and mind with us. Then the world might believe that You, in fact, sent me. John 17:21 MSG*. As we look at the quarter century behind us, we see an impact anchored in pursuing and growing in oneness and seeking kingdom partnerships for His glory.

Partnership first with God is the central anchor of our work and family. It all goes back to the day at break-time in my standard three class when a fellow student led me to Christ. The encounter with Jesus Christ progressively shaped my perspective of dependency on one another. I later identified my purpose, linked to a missional call. I completely surrendered to God and the pursuit of this call. That meant dethroning self and enthroning Christ to use me as He would, for whatever and however He chose. Partnership with Him and with those He brings my way, was planted in me. In discernment, I submit all relationships to Him.

While in medical school, where I met my future husband, Festus, I shared with him how I was already in covenant with God. In response to his marriage proposal, I asked him to first consider if the missional call would then become our joint purpose. He was willing to do this, and we launched into a life long journey of growing in partnership. We got married after my graduation, proceeded to establish a family, a home and grow in our careers with an intent to be equipped and trained for missions.

When the appointed time came, we jointly made the decision to go. As a family, we committed to pursuing missions as a life vocation. Our call was to Ethiopia but we first served among the Maasai in Kenya for 18 months before we moved on to what we knew would be a life-long work, starting from Ethiopia. That initial time among the Maasai gave us a chance to be set apart from the social norm: pilot, adjust and position ourselves and the family to work together. Our family micro-culture became what we have moved with and practised wherever we have served in the nations.

The fruit of this partnership is LIA. Life in Abundance International serves the poor and the vulnerable to address the root causes of poverty, leaving a legacy of sustained transformational development in communities. The work first started in Ethiopia where we went as cross-cultural missionaries and today, LIA works in 12 countries in Africa, and two in the Caribbean, and has support offices in the US, UK and Switzerland. LIA also has an Aviation Ministry that supports the work as well as two training centers that equip leaders for wholistic ministry[90].

Over the years our partnership grew to encompass aspects related to each of our specific giftings and experiences. While at the beginning, Festus functioned as administrator for the medical ministry in Ethiopia, over time he was called to his own areas of ministry. In 2001, Festus felt called to study Missiology at Fuller Seminary while we were in the US and the whole family moved to California to support those studies. God used that time to also grow my ministry with LIA by connecting me with like-minded people who helped me set up LIA as a non-profit in the United States. Sometimes we have worked in dual assignments taking up opportunities. When we returned to Ethiopia, Festus was called to lead another organization while I took on the role of LIA President and CEO, as the Board encouraged me.

Today, I lead Life In Abundance as the Founder and Festus supports me as my spouse. At home, I am a wife and mother. I relate to Festus as my leader and the head of the household, submitting in honour to him and serving him in my role as a wife. This has released both of us to serve from a secure base. He serves as an adjunct professor in leadership development.

Our allegiance to God first and then to each other has influenced our decisions and developed our marriage and ministry. This order has provided cover, protection and nurture. God commands a blessing that fosters peace and joy, and makes us a blessing.

How wonderful, how beautiful, when brothers and sisters get along!
Ps 133:1 MSG

---

[90] The author shares more of this story in her book, The Pursuit of His Calling: Following in Purpose.

Unity, To Let the World Know!

Leslie and Chad Segraves

We met and married in six months, and lived happily ever after ... Well, not exactly.

On our wedding bands, we engraved Jn 17:23, *"May they be brought to complete unity, to let the world know."* At that time, we didn't understand how much this verse would guide our marriage, parenting, and ministry.

Soon after marrying, some deep struggles emerged because both of us had goals, strong personalities, and similar leadership gifts. What did it mean to partner together as a man and woman serving God? Though surrounded by people who believed "men lead, and women assist," we felt the Lord say, *"You will know the Truth, and the Truth will set you free."* We set our hearts on Jesus; wondering if God would reveal A. God-designed male hierarchy or B. a different leadership model?

Loving Jesus meant honouring God's Word – so we began deep theological reflection. We studied biblical cultures, contexts, and languages. We asked questions. We prayed and sought to understand God's heart and kingdom. Over time, we discovered that God wants godly men and women to serve side-by-side and shoulder-to-shoulder as they reflect God's glory, God's peace, and God's own unity within the Trinity.

A model to emulate

Early in our marriage, God gently prodded us to study the Trinity as a model for our marriage and ministry. Beautiful! The Bible reveals that the co-equal Persons of the Trinity prefer one another. Each mutually honors, serves, loves, yields, and submits to one another. The Trinity is not ranked in an eternal hierarchy of one-directional command/obedience. The Persons fully share authority and are unified in will. The Trinity is not defined by eternally fixed "roles." No Person of the Trinity is ranked before or after, greater or lesser. Throughout Scripture, we see full (or rather *perichoretic*) participation in the actions of the Other Persons.

God created male and female in His image in Genesis 1:27. Understanding more about the way relationship worked within the Trinity caused us to recognize the power of preferring one another, empowering one another, and working with one another. Even when living in India, the Middle East, or East Asia, we sought to prefer the other. When babies came along, we chose to both parent our kids and both continue to use our gifts in ministry. We chose to not fall into the model of "the man continues ministry, while the woman waits." Rather, together we serve. Together we raise children.

A commission to achieve

In Gen 1, God commanded both the man and woman to "be fruitful, multiply, fill, subdue, and rule" the earth. These commands parallel Jesus' commission in Mt 28. In no place does Jesus limit who should go, make disciples, baptize or teach. Both men and women are needed to complete God's great mission. Today there are still two billion people waiting to hear the Good News of Jesus for the first time. To reach the world, we need all of God's people equipped and empowered to use their gifts for His purposes!

As we grew to understand God's global heart, we formed an interdenominational non-profit ministry twenty years ago. We seek to cast hope among unreached people groups so everyone has a chance to hear of Christ, experience Christ, and multiply Christ in their own local contexts. By working with Asians (in unity), both tangible and spiritual needs have been met. We equip men and women to plant churches. Recognizing that women usually bear greater child responsibilities in Asia, we adjusted the equipping to accommodate their schedules. Thus far, in one area of Asia, we have equipped four thousand women to plant churches. They have planted thousands of house churches so far!

Theological minefields to avoid

As we labour in ministry, we have seen two polarized dangers to male/female partnership. One side uses Scripture to limit people God wants to release into leadership, and the other side's worldview on "equality/rights" causes them to condone actions that oppose God's character. Both sides hurt the Mission of the Church to make and grow new disciples who follow the teachings of Christ.

Side I:

Too Restrictive – God's heart beats for all people groups to know and worship Him. The harvest is plentiful, and the workers are few! Therefore, we should read and apply scripture from the perspective that encourages the multiplication of godly labourers. The Holy Spirit "looks at the heart" when gifting men and women (1 Sam 16:7). At what do we look?

Side 2:

Violates God's Character – Here we note two errors to avoid.

A. God is Holy (1 Pet 1:15-16, Is 6:3). Because God is Holy, all leaders should walk in godliness. Sadly, we have seen that some who open doors for women leaders in the Church categorize it under "equal rights" or "justice" and then also support ungodly sexual relationships.

B. God is Life (Jn 14:6, Acts 17:25). Because God is Life, both men and women should passionately protect unborn babies stamped with His image, and vulnerable people of all ages. Sadly, we have seen some who promote women in leadership also approve of abortion (again on the basis of "rights" or "reproductive justice").

Either of these minefields reflects badly on God's character, impacts God's mission, and hinders the call of the Church to be counter-cultural. However, we believe when men and women rise with a passion for God's holiness, God's value for life, and God's unity between men and women – then the world will desire and more deeply know and experience Christ.

Shoulder to shoulder

In our experience, when Christlike brothers and sisters labour together to extend God's Kingdom, reflecting the character and principles of His kingdom, they increase ministry impact and harvest more eternal fruit. May godly men and women run together in unity, side-by-side and shoulder-to-shoulder, to the lost world.

Working with Men and Women Takes More than a Smile

Evi Rodemann

Summer 2018, in the US. I was queuing for food among hundreds of conference goers, most of whom were men. The man behind me said "Hi" while we waited in the line and then startled me with a question: "And, you are the spouse of which leader here?"

I could not believe this to be a starter for a great conversation. Rapid thoughts floated to my mind. "Do I give him a straight answer as a good true German? Does my gender really tell who I am made to be?" I turned, smiled and said: "I belong to Jesus and I am a leader" and continued choosing my salad. He mumbled something, blushed and left the queue to mingle with other men.

Having been brought up in a Christian home, it had never really entered my mind until I became an adult, that I could not pursue what I felt called to. From an early age especially, my father invested into us seven girls and one boy intentionally and equally. We were free to choose any direction we felt we should take.

Hearing God's call

I became a Christian aged ten and felt called into missions at a big conference. At thirteen, I went on my first summer outreach trip helping with children's evangelism. At the age of sixteen, I was deeply inspired at a missions conference, and I organised a city outreach in my hometown a year later. At this time, refugees were flooding my city during the Balkan war and I started visiting them, got others on board and organised a Christmas party for them in the town hall. I was young, naive, only seventeen. Burdened by things that broke God's heart, I ventured out: never did it occur to me that I could not lead such things because of my gender.

Later, I studied missions and theology, and got engaged in various mission agencies and youth organisations. I had written down my personal mission statement when I was 23 years old and I pursue my dreams today, knowing that God has gifted and called me.

I have had opportunities to work and lead locally, then citywide, nationally, European and now, even globally, but I have never sought bigger platforms. I do not believe that this is how the Kingdom of God works. One of the highest values I am driven by is being faithful to what God has entrusted to me. And if leadership is one of the giftings, I need to be willing and available.

Some of my learnings on my leadership journey as a single female leader:

Know who you are and your stand on theology

To know who I am is of utmost importance: it is neither my position nor my calling but God who calls me his child.

From knowing who you are, which includes knowing and practising your God-given gifts, you will then need to figure out your theology on leadership, also as a woman.

The opinions of other leaders and theologians might be hard to handle sometimes, but to stand firm, knowing these two things will make us secure in following Jesus and in leading.

I encourage everyone, regardless of their theology, to speak about their beliefs so that we understand where everyone comes from. Often it is unwritten beliefs which make work together so much harder.

Dealing with jealousy

One of the things though I have encountered early on in leadership was jealousy. I have sometimes become a threat to men but also to the wives of leaders. Occasionally as a single woman I encountered some ugly situations as I worked closely with some male leaders. Some women feared for their marriage if their husband worked with another woman. Some men did not want to make space to lead, feeling I was taking a piece of their cake away.

Being single in this case made collaboration sometimes more challenging, but I tried to be direct and open, to reduce any issues.

Gender does not define what I can do

I don't make gender a big deal. For me, it is more important to defend gifts than gender.

I do not enter a room and scan how many men or women are gathered, neither do I check rings on fingers or not. For me and most leaders I have met, it is about the Kingdom of God. For sure, as leaders we need to always check our motivation for our leadership and get corrected, but most leaders are into Kingdom business. They long to see God come and do his work.

Some men may only work with women if there are no men around, but for most, they work with anyone who is called, and gender does not dictate what I cannot or can do.

Working together with dignity and respect

A high value for me is treating everyone with respect and dignity, no matter what their positions or theological views might be. And it pays off. I often hear from men how they appreciate working with and next to me. There have been moments where men came and apologized for not making space for us female leaders, where they perceived us as a threat or an intrusion. Sometimes even men I have worked with for a few years sought the conversation and I realise some men feel insecure working with women.

It is good when men understand that some female leaders need more encouragement to take on a position because they can withdraw easily when there are dominant men in the room. Sometimes I raise my voice and lead and sometimes I serve the coffee, not because I am a woman but because I want to serve my fellow leaders

Show grace

A few years ago, I was invited to speak at a European conference where about 300, mainly males, attended. It lasted 3 days and no one really talked to me until after the last session when I did a key presentation. Once I was done, I had a line of 20 men queuing up wanting to get my slides, connect and exchange business cards.

I wanted to scream and shake these men, but I chatted with God about it instead. Not only did he comfort me, but he also challenged me to extend grace, to smile and show grace. I did just that and took their business cards and followed up.

There are situations where women leaders are pushed to the side, are not taken seriously or where wrong assumptions are made. But it is not up to me to judge. I need to forgive and get on with life entering the doors God has opened for me.

Build healthy relationships

I have so benefited from many valuable friendships with other leaders, including men, and I have enjoyed exchanging ideas.

Yes, our over-sexed society makes it sometimes very hard for both sides just to be friends and develop healthy relationships with the opposite sex. But it is needed to lead well and together. I have developed some healthy guidelines for myself and have set my own boundaries to what a friendship with the opposite gender means. And in this, friendships flourish and are highly meaningful.

Some men seek my advice and counsel regularly. I seek counsel from various male leaders as well.

Have someone walk alongside

In my various leadership roles, I had been looking for a female mentor. I would have loved an older woman in leadership. Everyone I had asked was already taken or not interested. When I became the CEO of a European organisation, it was men who took me under their wings. One friend paid for a male mentor to walk with me for a year. At another period, my employer paid a male mentor to guide me through the leadership process.

When I encountered challenging situations in leadership, these men walked parts of the painful journey with me and always cheered me on. I owe them, and God, so much for where I am now.

I am sure God is guiding me and giving me opportunities. He is much more interested in my gifts and obedience than he is in my gender.

Men and Women Co-Working for God's Kingdom

Menchit Wong

"Why me?" is a question which evokes powerful emotion. It could be the cry of the girl child, a victim of cultural beliefs that prevent her from pursuing education, from enjoying the gift of childhood and that thrust her into early marriage with an elderly man. The same question could be heard from a frustrated woman, who is a gifted leader but could not be promoted in a company that believes men should be given the most senior management roles. And the same question could be heard, albeit very softly, from a young missionary woman, with dynamic skills and talents, who is relegated to routine tasks, year after year, because of the concern that if she is given roles that match her competence, she will outperform the young man being groomed as the next pastor of the local church.

In my personal experience, I found myself asking the same question throughout my thirty years of local and global ministry. I recall my first meeting with an international team of subject matter experts that I was tasked to lead. One of them said, "Let's pray for Menchit so that the Lord will teach her how to do her job." I knew that this Christian leader meant well, but deep in my heart, I felt awkward that he said it that way. At another time, I was literally pushed, shoved aside and yelled at by a senior pastor of a church where we were hosting a global conference. He wanted me to bring to the stage the next speaker who was still on her way. I felt shamed and dishonored for a small task. I wanted to leave my Organizing Committee tasks and fly home. Then I heard the still small voice of the Holy Spirit telling me, "now you know how a child who is marginalized and discriminated feels like. Now you can speak on their behalf with a more compelling voice."

But times, they are changing. The Holy Spirit is on the move. The Global Consultation for Women in Christian Leadership held in Amsterdam in 2019 issued The Call to affirm and celebrate the contribution of women in the work of the Gospel. And many men from all backgrounds have endorsed it.

Why not?

In the last twenty years of engagement in global child advocacy, I have seen the global Church rise up in obedience to God's call for recognizing the intrinsic worth and dignity of every child and every person as esteemed, encouraged and enabled co-workers for the work of the Kingdom. "Why not?" is the call for women to rise in greater strength for partnership in global mission.

What has esteemed, encouraged, and enabled global partnership? It is Spirit-led partnership of men and women demonstrated by **affirmation, appropriate application, and activation of their complementary strengths for the work of the Kingdom.**

Let me go back to the story of the Christian leader who prayed that God would teach me how to do my job. At my first meeting with this team of accomplished men, I recognized each of their expertise. I also affirmed what mine was. These men were outstanding individual contributors. They needed a leader with skills in facilitation, relational skills and a strategic mindset that could synergize their expertise in advocating for children in poverty to the Global Church. Serving as leader for this international team was truly humbling and made me more prayerful. The rallying cry in my head was: identify each one's specific valuable contribution, bring integration by strategic application of each one's particular gifting, facilitate activities in a humble but firm approach, and do everything with team consensus, prayer and a spirit of unity. I was involved in this global team for a little over ten years. By God's grace, this strong partnership of men and a woman paved the way to develop and implement child protection policy across our organization serving twenty-six countries. This partnership produced at least two books, inspired the creation of a training center for children's ministry workers in a continent, and ignited a global alliance to advance holistic child development among local churches, denominations, and theological and academic institutions. This same team helped lead and organize the first global consultation that produced the Lausanne Occasional Paper on children-at-risk.

What if?

Imagine a world where people are valued for their unique strengths, not demeaned because of differences and weaknesses. How might partnership look if we affirm and value individual skills and talents, appropriately apply these individual skills to the tasks required, and activate the team with a humble, prayerful, and united spirit in Christ. I believe these are some keys to fruitful partnership. I invite our brothers and sisters all over the world to esteem, encourage, and enable one another in the work of the Kingdom.

Life in Partnership

Emma and Andy Dipper

When we think of partnership, we believe that we are both God's image bearers of equal value and of equal beauty! Which means that our partnership at its best, shows God to those around us.

We are very comfortable being husband and wife, first modelled in the Garden. Eve was Adam's Ezer or Helper. We see this relationship as equitable. God is described far more as Ezer or helper than Eve throughout scripture and as we walk through our marriage, we long to be effective helpers to one another.

In reality it means playing to the strengths of one another and wanting the best for each other, so we become an effective team in family and ministry. Most of the time we have had the opportunity to co-work in similar fields of ministry. And where we work separately, we welcome the other in. For example, Andy is part of Emma's team in Gender and Religious Freedom as his contribution needs to be recognised, and is greatly valued by the whole team.

Working in partnership can be risky. We externally process our thoughts and opinions so people see our marriage in action and we have to be comfortable to disagree publicly. It's part of growing and developing. However, disagreeing is different to criticism and we avoid doing that in public. We seek to create space for the other to flourish and we now have ease to critique and give honest feedback to one another.

We tend to have 'departments' where we know the other is more comfortable and competent. Andy naturally has the skills with our technology and finance. Emma is competent in health and organisation of people, events and the household. If we are requested to lead and preach at a church service, Andy will lead and organise the worship and Emma will preach. These are our more comfortable places to serve.

As the years have progressed, we recognise how we have become a 'tag team' when dealing with multiple issues in community and pastoral crises: we trust the other to say the right thing or to use the silences. We like to explore different models of leading: we want to keep pushing and offering an example of partnership in leadership that can encourage organisations to 'risk' new things.

As we are both natural and trained leaders, there are significant challenges. But over time, we recognised the need to keep listening, learning and trusting each other. Emma has sold a house whilst Andy was in Iraq without being able to contact him. Andy did a great 'engineering job' on our youngest daughter's lip with some strips of plaster when she had a very bad cut, whilst Emma was away.

When Andy is constructing sheds and doing other heavy work, he enlists the help of his daughters who are competent and generally lighter when it comes to securing roof panels! Our daughters know that when they leave the family home and make their own home, they depart with a full first aid kit, some recipe books and a good tool kit. We don't expect them to 'wait for a man to help,' but simply ask who might be available, be they male or female.

We have seen parenting as a partnership since the birth of our first child. However, the natural rhythm of pregnancy and childbirth meant that our roles were much more polarised when we had young children and babies. As they grew, so did Andy's ability to engage practically. He has always tried to connect emotionally and be there at bedtimes from the beginning.

We made the decision to be the primary care-givers for our daughters. This has had an effect on our finances and on Emma's ability to seek paid employment and senior roles even when the children were older. We have relied on Andy for his income and that has meant he has sometimes missed out on family time and felt the pressure 'to provide.' We recognise that this is as much down to our cultural backgrounds as well as and the practicalities of family life.

When we have worked in other cultures, we have tried to be respectful but over time we were willing to be counter cultural with some level of courage (or foolishness). When we were in Afghanistan, the Taliban were in government, and we both attended meetings and negotiations as we wanted to show in that context, how Andy honoured Emma as an equal. We had a mixed response!

We have three daughters. We have not always honoured each other as we should and we have fallen into the trap of gender stereotypes. For example, our youngest daughter wants to study as a physicist. She lacks the skills and practice in dealing with mechanics as she never had mechanical toys as a child, and she can see the boys in her class have a very different approach.

Gender stereotypes are sometimes used in the interpretation of scripture and this grieves us. But what is important to recognise is how intensely angry and disenfranchised our daughters and their Christian friends are about those stereotypes. They get angry that a woman may be stopped from reaching her full potential due to gender; but they also see that men are locked into a toxic masculinity where they are perceived as weak if they dare to serve with compassion or gentleness, or give 'power' away. We honestly believe that we will lose the next generation if we keep arguing over the roles and leadership of men and women.

We love that God has created us male and female and we celebrate what each brings. As we grow older, wiser and even greyer, we pray that our grandchildren will learn, serve, nurture and lead in ways that celebrate and model the wonderfully diverse and unified trinity of God the Father, Son and Holy Spirit and not be limited by their gender or expectations placed upon them.

Singleness and Marriage

Alison Guinness

I grew up in a non-Christian family where the expectation of my parents was that I should marry someone who had a good career, ideally a doctor or a lawyer, and we should thereafter live in a quiet part of the south of England and not seek to do anything too out of the ordinary with our lives. Whilst I rejected some of these values, due to my Christian faith, the desire to get married was very influential in my thinking. When many of my peers in the Christian Union got engaged at university, aged about 20, I felt very left out.

It's really only with the benefit of hindsight that I can truly see that God had bigger plans for me. I can see that had I got married when I was very young, I may have followed in the footsteps of my parents' marriage which has not really been an equal partnership; they were from very different social backgrounds and in their marriage my mother dutifully followed my father around the world and hosted his official guests, when he was a station commander, in his role as an officer in the Royal Air Force. My father, an only child, had been brought up in India, his own parents being the third generation of their respective families to live there, with servants and a country retreat. He'd attended expensive schools and was adventurous and loved rowing; my mother was one of four children, whose parents were ordinary hard working folks. My mother didn't share many interests with my father. My parents were not believers and their marriage was not intentional for the Kingdom of God.

Some wonderful older Christian couples and singles invested in my life from my mid-teens onwards and made a deep impression on me – particularly in how they lived their lives in partnership. I saw how both the husband and wife in these couples seemed to flourish more than they may have done without each other.

I am thankful to have been part of a dynamic church movement in SE London during my 20's which really encouraged women and young people in leadership. Alongside this, I began visiting Burundi in East Africa. Having first felt called to work in that region of Africa in my late teens, I became convinced this is what God had for me next. However my parents were saying that if I went to Burundi I would never get married, have children, own a house or have a pension! It was a battle to choose between pursuing what I understood to be my calling and remaining in England. In the end, I became convinced through the testimony of Shadrack, Meshach and Abednego in Daniel 3:17-18, that God was more than able to do a miracle for me, but even if He didn't, I was not going to bow down and worship other gods.

Looking back on my early years in Burundi, as a single white woman with mostly male Burundian colleagues, it was overall a positive experience. The hardest part was the loneliness of being single. I was at times treated as an 'honorary man', given that I was white and sadly treated with greater respect than many Burundian women were, but as I look back, I have much gratitude to my Burundian colleagues for the way in which they worked with me. I recognise that they gave me more leadership opportunities than I may have had at the same stage of life had I remained in the UK. You might say that the leadership style was quite prescriptive in how I was delegated responsibility to lead and work with others in the trauma healing programme. However I was also seeking to come under Burundian leadership so I accepted this.

There was a point where the loneliness and challenges of living in Burundi started to make me feel very discouraged. I took a retreat and felt God say that rather than stop working in Burundi, I should take a year out and study at All Nations Christian College. This was a wonderful, refreshing, albeit challenging time. Towards the end of the academic year, as I was about to turn 35 my parents said, 'If you go back to Burundi it'll be the nail in the coffin of you ever getting married and having children'. I took another retreat and felt God speak to me from Sarai and Abram's story in Genesis 16. They couldn't see how God would fulfil His promises to them and Abram ended up sleeping with Hagar and Ishmael was conceived. I felt God saying to me that it is better to trust Him than to try to work things out for ourselves. So I returned to Burundi and continued working there. It was another year before I met Paul, to whom I am now married.

As I reflect on my marriage, compared with what it might have looked like, had I married in my early twenties, I notice a number of things. Firstly, Paul and I met in Burundi doing what we had both felt called to do. We never had to make any compromise to our calling. Secondly and perhaps most significantly, the years prior to meeting Paul were not altogether easy but they shaped whom I have become today. I had the time to pursue leadership opportunities. It therefore felt obvious that we should become partners together for God's Kingdom, that we would both continue to be involved in ministry and as a result, we would seek to share parenting. It is not easy but we both recognise that between us we have so much more to offer than either of us does individually. In many ways we feel happier and healthier in marriage than we did before though there have also been some challenging times – particularly when we combined finishing MA studies with having babies.

If we had married younger, we wouldn't necessarily have chosen to have so much change in such quick succession (marriage, our first baby 10 months' later, two more babies within 5 years on top of 2 Masters' courses, travelling and learning how to share our work and parenting!) but we are walking the journey together and grateful for that.

Our life in missions has helped us in learning to talk things through. It may have helped that Paul's mother had held a significant career in helping him see that it is possible. Paul has attention deficit disorder and struggles to remember small details or stay focussed on things which don't excite him. As a result I have taken on the bulk of our personal and work admin which although I am efficient in doing, has sometimes caused me to feel resentful – it can feel it is all I do. It is an issue we discuss quite regularly so that I do get to do work which interests me. Paul has been very supportive of my roles as Vice Chair of the Board of All Nations Christian College, UK and on the board of a bible college in Burundi. As we look back to what we both experienced when we were younger, it has helped shape us into who we are today. To God be the glory!

Partnering as a Single Woman

Amy Summerfield

Young and single

The first time I was presented with the prospect of leading a church by my long-term mentor and leader of the church network, we both burst out laughing. I was to become the first solo pastor of the network, breaking the husband/wife team model. It all seemed ludicrous – at 32 years old with no formal training and a massive educational and academic battle due to dyslexia – the odds weren't great.

In my favour was a fearless passion for God and His people, expressed through the leadership gift on my life, along with years of children's and youth ministry. This proved vital as the church I was to lead had experienced serious safeguarding issues for which the previous pastor had been dismissed. The prospect of moving to Scotland away from family and friends to a church about to face a public court case wasn't attractive, but there was something appealing about swimming against the tide as the first single female leader in the network and I knew I could help the church through the trauma it had experienced.

Leading as a single woman

In my 20 years of being a female leader, I have faced opposition and even abuse. I've experienced people walking out as I preached, I've been told I would never be respected, and that I was only permitted to preach because I was a youth worker. One couple threatened to stop tithing if I was allowed to preach any more. More shockingly, being young and single caused men to feel they could inappropriately touch me. At times I have had to make formal complaints, which was heartbreaking for all, but necessary to address archaic church culture that has not trusted or treated women well.

Egalitarian values were intrinsic in the network of churches where I led, creating a pathway for my leadership. The men in the church held space for me, and the church protected and persevered with and for me. Although there were challenges as people faced up to their deep biases, I loved the ease and acceptance I received when speaking as their pastor to the men's events, talking about issues like purity.

But unconscious bias is still common. At a regular ecumenical event with all the churches in the district I was announced as the speaker for the next meeting, followed by 'Men, you don't have to come if you don't want to.' I was assured it was meant as a joke. I have been asked 'Whose wife are you?' and my assertion of 'Actually I'm the pastor, and I'm single,' would be met with raised eyebrows, or comments like, 'Oh, good for you,' or 'You're brave.'

Crazy questions abound! Don't you want to be married? It must be hard for you with all these children in the church. I was asked a couple of times if I was a lesbian. I have also been questioned about any previous hidden sin which might block my opportunity to be married (which presupposes that every married person doesn't have such sin to deal with). Such comments are clumsy and thoughtless. There have been occasions when, with no prior warning, I've been publicly prayed for about marriage and kids, which is exceedingly presumptuous, and I have fumed inside. I do wonder whether single men get the same comments and judgement.

It's so important to give single leaders the choice in this subject. If they want to talk the issues through with someone, they will.

Loneliness

The Church's focus on marriage and family is difficult for singles to navigate and leadership loneliness is intensified. The lack of having someone to run things by is tough, and you can't always talk things through with your team. This is highlighted at ministry events where I have often been the only woman, or one of very few women. It takes determination to attend these events with resilience and strength.

Working with men

As a single woman working alongside men, I began to understand there were different kinds of colleagues:

POSITIVE – Thankfully there are a growing number of men who are supportive and encouraging of women leaders. They do not make unnecessary 'concessions' and they genuinely include women and value them as equals.

PROTECTIVE – their chivalry was expressed by wanting to do the driving, the heavy lifting or door opening. Although admirable, there were times when such actions provoked an inward battle because I felt the need to prove I was quite capable of doing it myself.

Maybe I'm stubborn, but I'm also a strong, confident woman who wants to model a 'can-do' mentality.

PREJUDICED – Across the wider Church and cross-denominational communities, prejudice was too common. Incalculable times I have been cut off when speaking or praying. I have experienced meanness and a fair amount of mansplaining along the way! I have been deleted from the agenda and sometimes not even invited to meetings. However, there's been a good outcome as I have learned to respond lovingly with grace while continuing to put my thoughts forward and believe for change. Over time, many of these behaviours changed as I responded well and I have made friends.

PREDATORY – I have also experienced abusive behaviour – attempted grooming, flirting, and inappropriate touch. This must and will change as more single women and men are released to lead in churches safely and with support.

I don't regret the leadership path I chose, and I'm excited at the way pathways continue to unlock for woman leaders. Both Jesus and Paul were single during their ministry recorded in the Bible. Being single was not described as a "Plan B," or as a transitional stage of life.

Single women leaders are still few and far between, but it is my hope that what I have experienced can be an encouragement to others, and that we will continue to see shifts in the Church that make space for women leaders. By the grace of God and through His anointing we've come a long way, but there's further to go if we are to fully include women, single or married, young or older, and from all ethnic backgrounds in all aspects of leadership in the Church.

Paving the Way for Other Women

Madleine Sara

Since the Palestinian church lives within a Middle Eastern worldview where hierarchy is part of the culture, we are segregated in terms of ministries and roles in churches. This has always created confusion and lack of clarity in how men and women relate to one another in ministry and leadership.

In order to reduce the gender gap and the social stereotypes that exist in the Palestinian church, I would like to see more cooperation and some kind of partnership. The church would benefit from the diversity of both men and women serving together. Therefore, we need to create ways for men and women to serve together on teams within the church. This includes developing a new inclusive culture where women's leadership skills would be invited, cultivated, utilized and appreciated.

The example of Jesus

Jesus left us several examples of how he valued and related with women. He had healthy relationships with the women who served alongside him. There were always women around Jesus. Jesus' behaviour was a constant challenge to the traditions, religious law and attitudes of the time regarding women in a male dominant culture.

Jesus affirmed women as he honoured and encouraged their faith, gave them dignity and value, and spoke to them in a positive manner. More than this, Jesus liberated them to be an integral part of the ministry and allowed women to travel with Him as companions. He laid a sure foundation during the three years of His ministry on the earth for their release as valued witness, teachers and leaders in the emerging Christian church.

Jesus had women disciples, women thinkers and women evangelists. "With Him went the Twelve, as well as certain women . . . Mary . . . Johanna . . . Susanna; and many others . . . who provided for them out of their resources" (Luke 8:1-3). We remember also the story of Mary and Martha. Martha took the typical woman's role (Luke 10:39-40). Mary, however, took a non-female role when she sat to listen and learn.

The first evangelist recorded in the New Testament was the Samaritan woman at the well with whom he had a theological discussion. Not only was she a woman, but a Samaritan. How did Jesus relate to her? He invited her into a conversation about worship, and he revealed to her that he was the Messiah. This confession of Jesus' true calling (John 4:26) is not found anywhere else yet in his public ministry. Culturally, Jesus contested norms. Although the culture dismissed the testimony of women, Jesus clearly chose women as the first witnesses of the resurrection. Through his actions, Jesus taught a lesson in inclusion and about who should be allowed to lead in his kingdom.

The way in which Jesus related to women, especially considering the background of Judaism, was revolutionary. Reading the gospels, there is evidence of Jesus' effect on the writings: Luke's Gospel has a special emphasis on the place of women; it is apparent that Christ viewed women as women, not as sex objects nor as sinful temptation.

Paving the way for women in the church

Finally, it is my desire to see the church moving towards involving women in leadership roles. My hope for the Palestinian church is to see more women stand up to be educated and empowered to challenge the unintentional oppressive culture. I see myself as Moses, preparing a new generation of believers and leaders, to enter the promised land, and expanding the kingdom of God by all means and giftings they were given by our mighty Lord. I see myself as Deborah, a prophetic voice, calling for male leaders such as Barak; and walking the war field together. I see myself as Naomi, mentoring young women and guiding them into their destiny. I see myself as Priscilla leading a church with her husband. I see myself as Phoebe, leading and being a co-worker to male leaders such as Paul – helping in planting churches, and being a patron and servant to the church.

For this to happen, I believe that we also need courageous male leaders to be part of this change. We need a new setting where shared leadership and decision making, theology and spirituality, give visibility to women's perspectives. It is about time that the Palestinian churches took actions in solidarity with women. We need to see women and men working alongside each other to allow for a new and different narrative, to create a community of oneness between men and women, and thus write a new scenario of history for the generations to come.

One of the greatest privileges I have had in my life is my husband Jack. Jack is a pastor, president of a college and an influential leader locally and globally. He is also considered one of the few pioneer leaders in the region supporting gender equality and creating a community of oneness between men and women. He is a leader who has advocated for women. I am blessed and honoured to be married to such a leader who has led this movement.

We need more male advocates so the church can reshape its patriarchal opinions regarding women in ministry before we step further to official ministry offices.

Here are some practical recommendations I have seen Jack and other male leaders use in this context:

1. Contextualised theology: in order to tackle the issue of women constructively, conservative Christians should further consider the contextual elements involved in both the church and New Testament theology.
2. Male leaders should deliberately make women visible to the church by affirming their gifts. There are usually opportunities for ministry and lay leadership. Has a woman done a significant role or ministry behind the scenes? We need to make sure to thank her and affirm her from the pulpit. Women should be called to pray or even lead the communion, share testimonies, and read Scriptures from the front of the church.
3. Diversify the staff and the leadership ministry to include women. Leadership in the church should aim to include gifted, experienced, educated and competent women leaders on the board or the leadership team.
4. Include women leaders who are gifted in preaching to the program of preaching.

May we raise up many more Deborahs, Naomis, Phoebes and Priscillas!

The Journey of Learning

All of us are learning and we don't stop! We want to pause and reflect on these stories.

What did you enjoy most about Gabriel and Jeanette's ideas in their chapter which introduces the stories section?

Culture

Our stories come from a mix of cultures: the UK – Emma and Andy, and Amy; Germany – Evi; Kenya – Florence; USA/Thailand – Leslie and Chad; Philippines and international – Menchit; Israel/Palestine – Madleine; UK/Burundi – Alison; USA/Latin America – Jeanette and Gabriel.

- In some of the stories, culture and Kingdom values are incompatible. How have the writers overcome those differences?
- How do you see culture and Kingdom values working together in a positive way in some of the stories?

Mutuality

A number of Christian writers like to talk about 'mutuality' in relationships – where all relationships in work and home life are for the mutual benefit of both men and women. Words like sharing, gifting and submission are all mutual expressions.

- Which stories talk about this and what can the writers teach us?

Co-workers

- What practical advice did you pick up that will help you to co-work with men and women more effectively?

A Final Word: Let Us Love One Another and Finish Well

Jay Matenga

The great divide

Humans are complex beings. We do ourselves a disservice when we surrender to reductionist definitions, assessing others according to simplistic stereotypes, to avoid the hard work of learning the glorious uniqueness that has been invested in each manifestation of God's image. We are all guilty of thinking along the lines of, "He's black, and black people are...", "She's attractive, therefore...", "They're fat, so they must...", "He's got great charisma, so let's ...", "She has too much to say for herself, so we need to ensure...", or similar.

We make judgements. Judgements lead to actions. Actions can either amplify or diminish the dignity of God's good creation. This process is core to our nature, but prejudging people according to tropes and stereotypes is a lazy and ungodly habit of the human race. We all do it. Some of us are more aware of it than others. Some of us are more restrained in our prejudice-informed actions than others. We are, however, all prone to judgementalism, for this is the root of sin—the knowledge of good and evil. Our ancestors ate from the source and we now sit as gods of our worlds with the untethered ability to decide what is acceptable and what is not, and then to autonomously determine how we will respond—to make or break a relationship with the 'other'.

With reference to human beings, the Psalmist declares that God's creativity is marvellous and "wonderfully complex" (Psalm 139:14 NLT). We are made in God's image, as Peirong Lin and others have previously pointed out. We are, each one, precious to our Creator. Our connection to God is jealously guarded by God, hotly contested by the adversary, and too easily taken for granted by each one of us. The promise of God's presence with us (and us with God) reverberates throughout Scripture as the supreme aim of the reconciling mission of God. Yet, the lamenting prophet speaks of our Lord grieving, "The human heart is the most deceitful of all things, and desperately wicked. Who really knows how bad it is?" (Jeremiah 17:9 NLT). To which, the Lord answers, "I, the LORD, search all hearts and examine secret motives." (Jeremiah 17:10 NLT); with consequences that follow. Beware: the Lord knows our motives.

At the conclusion of our Creator's six-phase genesis act, all things were declared superb. God rested and was pleased with the presence of the humans, who were commissioned to tend the pristine new world. They were two types of the same species: male and female. Being made wonderfully complex relates in part to our respective biologies—"You made all the delicate, inner parts of my body and knit me together in my mother's womb." (Psalm 139:13 NLT)—but biology is only one dimension of our complexity. Every person has distinct bodily mechanisms, functions, systems and innate preferences that make up our whole. Two sexes are normative for our species. Normative, but by no means simple. Members of each sex share common, but not identical complexity. We are, each one, *wonderfully* complex beings. Our biology is influenced by generations of genetic adaptations, emerging into social contexts that further shape who we are, how we think, what we do, and the limits of plausibility for our place of belonging. We are born into a group of people, family, community, society and nation, in a specific time and space that we come to know as our gendered lived reality—for better or for worse.

Exasperated by his own embodied experience, the Apostle Pauls exclaims,

> *"I have discovered this principle of life—that when I want to do what is right, I inevitably do what is wrong. I love God's law with all my heart. But there is another power within me that is at war with my mind. This power makes me a slave to the sin that is still within me. Oh, what a miserable person I am! Who will free me from this life that is dominated by sin and death?" (Romans 7:21-24).*

The malevolent power that vexed Paul haunts us all. It is the destructive influence of judgementalism, a 'will to knowledge'. It suggests that we can decide for ourselves what is good and what is bad, regardless of God's revealed standards. Even when we know what those standards are, we are too often inclined to do otherwise. And we impose our standards onto others, more often than not to the detriment of our relationships—no more so than our relationship with God.

No sooner had Paul flung his words out in despair, than he immediately answered his own question. Who will deliver us from our compulsion to abide by this malevolent judgemental force at work within us and our relationships? "Thank God! The answer is in Jesus Christ our Lord." (Romans 7:25a NLT). This short declaration of truth sums up all that Paul had been explaining to that point in his letter to the Romans, reiterating what he noted earlier, that "we can rejoice in our (plural) wonderful new relationship with God because our (plural) Lord Jesus Christ has made us (collectively) friends of God" (Romans 5:11 NLT). We, male and female, have our relationship with God restored in-Christ, and with it our relationship with all of those in-Christ with us. The great divide is healed. Our relationships can be reconciled. We can finally lay down our prejudice, judgementalism, expectations and strivings, and rest, allowing God to be God. We now live free to love one another as the fruit of God's rule and reign—to be one.

Becoming one

Unity is a grossly misunderstood concept. Too often it is interpreted through the grid of judgmentalism. Unity is thought only to be possible when everyone accepts the conditions of belonging that are established by the leaders of a group. If you do not behave a certain way, according to 'our' judgements, you do not belong; and, furthermore, you become the reason unity is threatened. This was the sin of the teachers of the law and the Pharisees. They had strict conditions for belonging to the people of God. Sure, those conditions were derived from Scripture, tradition (the Law) and accepted cultural mores, but they ignored "the more important aspects of the law—justice, mercy, and faith." (Matthew 23:23b NLT). In each of the four gospel narratives, Jesus illustrates a life led by the Spirit of God and the transcendent ethics of God's kingdom—where allegiance to God's Son (faith) manifests in loving kindness (mercy) to one another, in covenantal communities[91] that live and work to align their reality with what God determines is right (justice) as a witness to all.

Jesus did not adhere to a code created by humans, yet he completely fulfilled the expectations of God's right ways. Jesus did not stereotype those he met, but he saw their unique good and held them to that standard. As Rosalee Ewell brought to our attention, Jesus called to himself a diverse band of disciples who each tested the harmony of the group, but even the

---

[91] I prefer to speak of covenantal community because it emphasises the means by which we come together in-Christ (covenant) and allows for broader expressions of what it might look like to be a community rather than just a congregation. It opens the imagination. Since the New Testament authors use multiple metaphors to express our unity in-Christ, I try to avoid using ἐκκλησία (ekklēsia), which (in English) we commonly call "the church", because of the institutional assumptions associated with the term. Institutional order is a gift from God and has its place, but constraining our cooperative relationships to a particular time, space and order can be another way we limit the potential of the lives we are meant to live, together, in-Christ.

betrayer was included until he chose to separate himself from the group. While the culture expected disciples to be male, the evidence is clear that Jesus was not constrained by the expectations of his time and place. Margaret Mowczko and Amanda Jackson ably pointed out that many women were among those who followed him, served him, and were *loved* by him ... as uncomfortable as that might seem from a hyper-sexualised context's perspective.

Jesus' acceptance of both male and female among his number was not unusual for God. While it might be hard for some to see, the entire biblical record elevates the role of women in myriad ways, many times contrary to social norms. We should all have been suitably chastised by Mary Evans when she pointed out that the role of women in the Bible is too often overlooked. Where we stand will always determine what we see, and the fact that Western theology has failed to give women their due in the biblical narrative is the biased result of reading Scripture with patriarchal eyes. As Andrew Bartlett indicated, we cannot help but read Scripture from our own cultural context, but that does not mean we need to stay there and 'hold the line' in defence of our reading, our judgements on the text. Jesus scolded the teachers of the law and the Pharisees for that kind of arrogance.

In contrast to uniformity, the unity of the kingdom of God is best described as diversity in constant tension. I use John 17:18-26 as my central missions text, which I call "The Great Commitment". I chose those specific verses because they begin with Jesus speaking of the Father's sending of the Son, explain what that sending looks like, and conclude with God being glorified as the objective of the sending. Missions influencers frequently reference the Father's sending of the Son (usually preferring John 20:21) and invent all manner of means and methods of sending from other parts of the Bible, yet completely ignore the fact that Jesus clearly stipulated the 'how'—integrated unity. See here, Jesus prayed "... may they be (integrated) in us so that the world will believe you sent me" (John 17:21 NLT). The only method by which the world will believe and know that the Father sent the Son, is our loving unity. Our participation, together, in God's mission is fully dependent on us understanding this and living it out in the world.

The communal reality of our life in-Christ cannot be overstated. Miroslav Volf is worth quoting in this regard,

> Because the Christian God is not a lonely God, but rather a communion of three persons, faith leads human beings into the divine communion. One cannot, however, have a self-enclosed communion with the Triune God—a

"foursome," as it were—for the Christian God is not a private deity. Communion with this God is at once also communion with those others who have entrusted themselves in faith to the same God. Hence one and the same act of faith places a person into a new relationship both with God and with all others who stand in communion with God. (Volf 1998, 173.)

We do not dwell in-Christ alone. We are part of a glorious collective, and it is into this ecology of relationships that we are saved—from isolation to communion. Volf goes on to affirm that we should not reduce our interconnectedness to the realm of mystical union. It is a bodily-experienced, interpersonal and sociological reality. In-Christ we are of the same family, convenantally tied, equally loved, called and equipped for our service to one another, and therefore God, in the world. Our relationships with one another, within and across the spectrum of global expressions of the faith, is an expression of worship. Paul makes this clear in Romans 12:1-2, when read through a covenantal-relationship lens and placed in the context of the whole chapter (and book). We automatically bring our preconceived ideas of worship into our reading of the text, but in context Paul is saying that our holy and acceptable sacrifice is a life lived in deference to one another, positioning our bodies in such a way that others are preferred. Our love for one another, as an expression of our worship of God, runs counter to the selfish, judgemental and (often) relationally-destructive behaviours and customs (patterns) of this world, and it is our Holy Spirit-empowered interpersonal relationships with one another in-Christ that transform our ways of knowing, thinking and being—our very person. That each of us is literally shaped through our interactive relationships is a matter of science that interpersonal neurobiology is confirming.[92]

Earlier, Rosalee Ewell wrote, "The journey of discipleship is one of getting closer to Jesus. As we get closer to Jesus we get closer to one another, and this is not always easy." It will be apparent to every believer everywhere that being drawn closer together in-Christ does not automatically translate into an experience of interpersonal bliss. Conflict is part of our lived experience and it does not cease when we step "out of the darkness into his wonderful light" (1 Peter 2:9 NLT), but it is redeemed. Christ's light, among other things, reveals truth. It both exposes our personal darkness, which emerges in relationship tension, and highlights God's goodness

---

[92] For an introduction to interpersonal neurobiology and its theological implications, I recommend *"The Anatomy of the Soul"* by Dr Curt Thompson. A primary source for interpersonal neurobiology would be Dr Dan Siegel's *"The Developing Mind."*

within us as we contribute the best of who God made us to be to the flourishing of our community/ies of faith.

We need to accept that our covenantal commitment to one another in-Christ will be fraught with what James called, "troubles of any kind" (James 1:2 NLT). James was not referring to external opposition or persecution, he was preparing readers of his letter for the coming lesson on unity in diversity. In the case of James' letter, it was predominantly economic disparity. The tensions we experience with one another in-Christ are a normal part of our process of development as disciples. As we persevere in the faith (the belief that we are part of a covenantal community in-Christ) and don't break fellowship[93], it develops us and we mature. This process, best imagined as a spiral, continues until we reach perfection (which I read as resurrection, since death is the ultimate test of our faith). So, the reason James expects us to rejoice when experiencing hardship with one another is because it is shaping us into maturity, into the likeness of Christ.

Here is a trustworthy saying: you cannot have harmony without tension. I learnt this from tuning instruments. Just as it is impossible to strike a harmonic note on a slack instrument string, it is impossible to develop unity without tuning (but not necessarily resolving) the tensions in any given group. Tension is what transforms us. Alternative perspectives help us see a fuller picture. Giving way to each other, yielding, is our living sacrifice, holy and acceptable to God (see Romans 12:1-2). This is the essence of the attitude of Christ that Paul describes in Philippians 2: 5-11. Building on what Peirong Lin has already mentioned, Paul refers to Jesus as 'giving up' his divine privileges. Theologically, this process is known as "kenosis" after the Greek term (κενόω [kenoō]) that is usually translated "gave up". Theologians tend to wrestle with the technicalities of how and what Jesus gave up as God, but they miss the point made obvious in the passage—Jesus yielded his privileges as God *in order to* serve others sacrificially, God was pleased and Christ was rewarded and transformed. Hopefully you can see the resonance with Romans 12:1-2 here.

Our one-ness, integrated into God in-Christ, is meant to be a struggle. It is a rhythm of giving up our will to knowledge, our convictions about what is best. It is a mutual self-denial in covenantal relationship with one another, that prefers the 'other', that seeks the best for all, that lovingly serves, and, as the rest of Romans 12 testifies, creates space for others to

---

[93] Consider also, Ephesians 4:2-3: "Always be humble and gentle. Be patient with each other, making allowance for each other's faults because of your love. Make every effort to keep yourselves united in the Spirit, binding yourselves together with peace." (NLT)

serve as they are gifted to do so. Preferring one another under tension is a process of perpetual reconciliation, sometimes getting our way, sometimes giving way, which results in the fellowship resonating with a harmony that transforms (or hybridizes) all participants. This interactive process is meant to happen at an interpersonal level and also on a macro level, globally. Afterall, Jesus' prayer for unity was not just for his immediate disciples, "but also for all who will ever believe in me through their message." (John 17:20 NLT)—regardless of the privileges or constraints of their identity, until the end of the age.

Serving in partnership

The kind of maturity the New Testament envisions for us in-Christ does not happen in groups where everyone is like us, and likes us. As uncomfortable as it is, our development as disciples and as covenantal communities in-Christ requires difference and tension—because the complex body of Christ is made up of myriad mechanisms, functions, systems and innate preferences all functioning together, as our love for one another permits others to contribute their gifts to the body (see 1 Corinthians 12:12-31*ff*). The entire New Testament (and, arguably, the whole canon) tells a story of strained relationships and the promise of perpetual (and ultimate) reconciliation in-Christ. Collectively, we have a ministry of reconciliation. Paul and his fellow servants exemplified this,

> *"So we have stopped evaluating others from a human point of view. At one time we thought of Christ merely from a human point of view. How differently we know him now! This means that anyone who belongs to Christ has become a new person. The old life is gone; a new life has begun! And all of this is a gift from God, who brought us back through Christ. And God has given us this task of reconciling people to him." (2 Corinthians 5:16-18 NLT).*

Note carefully Paul's surrender of judgementalism—once the prejudiced persecutor, he ceased evaluating people from a human point of view. He submitted to God's perspective. Everyone in-Christ is a new being, transcending the human categories that differentiate us. Regardless of the earthly categories we are born into, we are now no longer constrained by prescribed limits of our colour, culture or ethnicity, whether we're the employed or the entrepreneur, or biologically male or female (see Galatians 3:18). We are all free to participate as citizens of a different kingdom with different ethics, mores and expectations. We are all free to serve wherever and however God calls us, with whatever gifts the Holy Spirit has invested in us, for the flourishing of God's covenantal community in-Christ, for the benefit of wider society, and for God's glory. What enabled Paul and his cohort to think like this? It is no secret. He told us: "Christ's love controls us" (2 Corinthians 5:14a NLT).

Paul pleads, "As God's partners, we beg you not to accept this marvellous gift of God's kindness and then ignore it." (2 Corinthians 6:1 NLT). What gift? The gift of our transcendent being in-Christ. The patterns of this world simply are no longer valid. Our earthly categorisations, stereotypes and resultant behaviours are unacceptable. Why then do we ignore the gift and insist on applying worldly patterns? I suggest it is because we have not yet surrendered our will to knowledge, our judgementalism, to God. Until we do, and adopt God's perspective, the world will not believe and know that the Father lovingly sent the Son, because the evidence of this truth—our loving unity—is not being demonstrated to them.

Until now, I have attempted to illustrate the depth, strength and endurance of interpersonal relationships expected of us as we participate in covenantal communities in-Christ wherever we are located. Common English terms for non-familial collaboration between people include "fellowship", "team" and "partnership". The editors chose "partnership" to define the theme of this book, with the intention of encouraging greater equality for women as co-labourers with men in Christ, creating synergy.[94] A potential problem with the term "partnership", though, is the contractual and transactional assumptions it carries in common use in the English-speaking industrialised world. When we are constrained by English it limits our imagination. Partnership strongly implies a conditional agreement (contract) between two or more autonomous entities to achieve a common aim (transaction), with the inference that once the aim is achieved the partnership dissolves.

We need to dispel the myth that we are autonomous beings in-Christ. Instead, we enjoy an inseparable mystical union at a spiritual level with all in-Christ, which manifests as an indivisible relational union when the Spirit of God brings us together in a shared space and time. We are not autonomous partners, we are representatives of a unified whole. There is no contractual arrangement, we are bound by a covenantal commitment. We are not involved so much in transactions as we are in mutual reciprocity, where the only debt we will ever owe one another is love (see Romans 13:8).

---

[94] From the Greek word, συνεργός (synergos), which Paul uses to describe Timothy and Philemon as fellow labourers.

In his contribution, Samuel Okanlawon makes a strong case for freedom from patriarchal assumptions and the resultant abuses against women. His exegesis of Galatians 3:28 is robust and supports well a call for a holistic perspective of interdependence between men and women, and a theology of inclusivity. The union of which I speak is one of deep inclusivity where, regardless of difference, we enjoy freedoms to be and do in obedience to God, guided by the collective wisdom of the fellowship, wherein we discover the mind of Christ (1 Corinthians 2:16), which helps us discern God's good, pleasing and perfect will for each one of us and for all of us (Romans 12:2).

In agreement with Samuel Okanlawon, this requires the deconstruction of the systems that limit the full expression of the gifts of God, otherwise known as "the behaviours and customs of this world" (Romans 12:2a NLT). Paul exemplified what he meant by non-conformance to the world's patterns, and Marg Mowczko has already shown us how he led the way by including women among his co-labourers. Let us follow his example, as he followed Christ's (1 Corinthians 11:1). Learning from Andrew Bartlett's illustrations from history and the distortions that he highlighted that are at work today, we must always remain vigilant against overlaying our behaviours and customs, our judgementalisms, on the text. Partnership does not mean relegating participants to stereotyped roles. It should mean the freedom to fully participate as gifted, and to participate in the process of deciding how those gifts can contribute toward the flourishing of the covenantal community and its witness, locally and globally.

Until the end

While this book has focused on men and women in partnership, I see little theological distinction between types of difference. Paul used interchangeable sets of contrasting binaries at different times (see for example Galatians 3:28; 1 Corinthians 12:13; Colossians 3:11), but he intended his lists to be examples, not exhaustive. We can add so many more categories of people today whose dignity is diminished by society but elevated in-Christ. Sometimes Paul included male and female, sometimes not. The principle, however, remains the same. In-Christ, we transcend the categories dictated by our contexts and the prejudices that diminish, separate and destroy relationships and contribution potential.

Nevertheless, the purpose of this book was to focus specifically on our biological binary, to break down the biases that persist in the global church against creating space for women to fully participate, especially if they are gifted in ways deemed to be the exclusive role of males according to the behaviour and customs of a context. We risk far too much by excluding female participation at any level of engagement in the life of covenantal communities, wherever they are to be found. Furthermore, unintentional exclusion of women from spheres of influence is as tragic as intentional restriction. Rosemary Dewerse and Cathy Hine provide an excellent example of this in their critique of the 2016 book, *Reading the Bible Missionally*, edited by Michael Goheen. The book is a culmination of papers from a 2013 conference on the theme of "A Missional Reading of Scripture", which attracted some 700 participants.

Dewerse and Hine point out that the book showed "no evidence of the nuances and insights of (female) missional reading and application." (Dewerse & Hine 2020, 30). Their article in *Mission Studies* (the Journal of the International Association for Mission Studies) sought to rectify that omission. The value cannot be overstated of their "Stories of faithful Oceanic women interweave(ing) with those of God and of biblical women, offering their complexities to challenge assumptions and simplicities." (Dewerse and Hine 2020, 29). This is one of myriad examples of the contribution of women to the Church and missions that speak powerfully into the theme of this book and, as this book shows with its content and contributors, without women's voices articulating their perspectives we are impoverished. Potential for growth in the Body of Christ is stunted when a large proportion of its members are prohibited from functioning as they are gifted.

We still have a long way to go to see the good news of Christ's deliverance understood and benefitting many parts of the world. We need the whole body of Christ flourishing in global witness and women have crucial roles to play in this at all levels. It was with reference to the faith of a persistent widow—a marginalised woman—that resulted in Jesus wondering, "when the Son of Man returns, how many will he find on the earth who have faith?" (Luke 18:8 NLT). Remaining faithful until the end, requires that we release everyone to express their faith. Sadly, as indicated in this volume by Mary Evans, and by Dewerse and Hine in their article, the potential contribution of women is too easily overlooked. Women should not have to fight for a hearing or to make their best contribution to a covenantal community in-Christ. The onus is on existing leaders to make space for the overlooked, ignored or outright silenced to freely participate. That takes intentionality.

During the longest leadership position I have held to date (15 years), I led a small team of women, with brief periods where a male worked alongside us. I currently lead a cohort of five female and five male deputy leaders guiding a large global missions network. I have spent more than 25 years helping men and women find their place in missions and listened, heartbroken, to stories of limitations placed on women in their fields of service. Conversely, where they did find opportunities to lead, I have worked alongside very competent and gifted women in international leadership. As a CEO, I have been accountable to female board chairs (and I am still) and have had the privilege of serving on governing boards with female chairs and alongside fellow female board members. My most influential doctoral supervisor was a woman, and so is my executive coach. In 1990 I married the woman I built a life with. It would be impossible to overestimate what I have learned from my professional and personal friendships with women and how they have helped transform me as a person, as a leader, and as a disciple of Christ.

Until relatively recently, I cannot say my experience of working alongside, or for, women was intentional. In my local context, it is somewhat normative. I am from Aotearoa New Zealand, which was the first nation in the world to give women the opportunity to vote. We seem less resistant to women's opinions and contributions than many other cultures I've experienced. But I trace my innate respect for women's influence back to my indigenous heritage. Māori society is very egalitarian and, in many ways, matriarchal. Biological sex matters little in determining what role a person can play in tribal society. Positions are determined by recognised potential. Some of the biggest advances in race relations in our nation were led by Māori women. It helps that our language does not have many gendered pronouns. "Matua", parent or respected older person, can refer to a male or female, and we bring this perspective into our understanding of God as the Creator without gender. So when we pray the Lord's prayer, it begins, "E tō mātou Matua i te rangi . . ." (Our Parent in heaven . . .). This simple linguistic turn opens up underappreciated facets of God's character significantly. As contributors to this book have already implied, in a patriarchal, machismo world, influenced by domination and aggression, a feminine perspective on our understanding of God and Scripture is sorely needed.

On my desk I have a plaque given to me by the International Director of a mission organization that I served as a country leader. It simply reads, "Let's finish well". It represents the dying words of his father, the founder of the mission, "I want to finish well". It is safe to say we are closer to the return of Christ than we have ever been. Let us all finish well. Let us allow one another to serve in our giftedness so that the global body of Christ can flourish and attract new members with new gifts to contribute from new contexts. Let us not let fear of impropriety get in the way, but instead remain faithful to those we are bound to by unique vows. Let us resist temptation to exploit, exert power or abuse our relationships. Such actions are abhorrent to our covenantal commitment to one another in-Christ. Love demands otherwise.

When it comes to friendships with members of the opposite sex, men should heed the advice Paul left for his younger co-labourer Timothy, "Treat older women as you would your mother, and treat younger women with all purity as you would your own sisters." (1 Timothy 5:2 NLT). With the reverse for women, therein lies the key for healthy relationships in-Christ: siblinghood. In-Christ we are more than partners, we are family. A holy family whose ethic is love, which manifests as: "joy, peace, patience, kindness, goodness, faithfulness, gentleness, and self-control" (Galatians 5:22-23 NLT)[95]. It is "not jealous or boastful or proud or rude. It does not demand its own way. It is not irritable, and it keeps no record of being wronged. It does not rejoice about injustice but rejoices whenever the truth wins out. Love never gives up, never loses faith, is always hopeful, and endures through every circumstance." (1 Corinthians 13:4b-7 NLT). Because, "God is love, and all who live in love live in God, and God lives in them. And as we live in God, our love grows more perfect. So we will not be afraid on the day of judgment, but we can face him with confidence because we live like Jesus here in this world. Such love has no fear, because perfect love expels all fear." (1 John 4:16b-18a). So, men and women, let us love well to the end.

References:

Dewerse, R. and Hine, C. "Reading from Worlds under the Text: Oceanic Women in the missio Dei" in Mission Studies 37 (2020), Issue 1, Journal of the International Association for Mission Studies. Koninklijke Brill NV, Leiden, 2020.

Siegel, D. "The Developing Mind: How Relationships and the Brain Interact to Shape Who We Are". Guilford Press, New York NY, 2012.

Thompson, C. "The Anatomy of the Soul: Surprising Connections between Neuroscience and Spiritual Practices That Can Transform Your Life and Relationships". Tyndale House Publishers, Carrollton TX, 2010.

Volf, M. "After Our Likeness: The Church as the Image of the Trinity". William B. Eerdmans Publishing Company, Grand Rapids MI, 1998.

---

[95] The addition of a colon following "love: ..." is considered appropriate by some commentators since the fruit of the Spirit is singular in the Greek. It certainly fits when matched with other Pauline passages such as 1 Corinthians 13:4-7.

Actions we can Take

This book is designed to stimulate our intellect, our heart and our actions. As we aim to finish well, we urge you to earnestly review the practices around you and consider what actions you can take to model co-working and co-leading.

Here are some practical actions we can take, even if some of them may sound challenging.

1. Carefully look at the way male and female roles within the family work in your life and in your nation. We want to see a generation growing up where the girl-child and boy-child will share responsibilities (and accountability) equally. Perhaps some of the assumptions we make about boys and girls are rooted in tradition not in God's design for gender.
2. Ask all the preachers in your churches to consciously search out women in the Bible to use in their teaching. Encourage youth group leaders and children's pastors to read this book and then use the hidden and neglected stories of women alongside those of men.
3. Increase women's representation in the churches' decision-making bodies to be of equal number to that of the men. Even if you have strict rules about preaching or pastoring, there are many other roles that can be shared more equally. Then, we should all be willing to look again at breaking down barriers around leadership, based on the explanations of key scriptures given by a number of writers.
4. Male leaders can make time and space to listen to women and other marginalized groups on an equal basis and to learn from their perspectives. This is not always easy when you are used to having your views heard. Practically, what can you do in your context to encourage women as well as other marginalized people to contribute to church life based on gifting, not gender or family connections or social class?
5. If you are an older leader, actively champion and encourage women, stepping back so they can come forward. If you are asked to lead a meeting or speak at a conference, suggest a younger person and/or a woman instead. We need to be intentional and not slip into stereotypes when looking for talented, spiritual new leaders. We could use many excuses for sticking to the same practices but the Church can only grow stronger if all of us are using our gifting fully.

6. The Call to All Christians says, *"We recognize that our communities and leadership structures have not always been encouraging, freeing or even safe for women and girls, who are each valued and loved by God. We acknowledge that the pathways for women to serve as leaders in the global Church are limited, and this has prevented many from contributing to the Church in this way. We acknowledge that the Church has deeply hurt many women and girls, and not heard or acknowledged their pain."* These are hard words for all of us. Our church communities and organisations need to acknowledge past mistakes in the way women have been treated and put new ideas and policies in place to change the way things operate. We cannot tolerate abusive behaviour and we cannot cover-up its consequences.
7. It is vital for us all to be flexible in the way we see women's leadership. The number of women who stay single or who are single for a significant part of their life, is growing across the world. Women will have various roles and responsibilities over their lifetime and as a general rule live longer than men. Perhaps traditional groups and ministries need to change and adapt.
8. The stories in this book highlight ways for single women to flourish in Christian contexts as well as talking about healthy partnerships in marriage. Use the stories as a jumping-off point to consider how your church or organization can help women (and men) to flourish and contribute their leadership skills at all stages of life and in all spheres of society.

Call to All Christians[96]

Women from diverse backgrounds call on all Christians to listen to the voices of women and recognise their gifting, to ensure the effective witness of the Church to the transforming power of the Gospel.

We affirm that Jesus came that we may all have life and have it in all its fullness[97]. This Gospel transforms lives; the Bible affirms that Jesus called, accepted, healed and restored women. We commit to sharing and demonstrating this Good News; women and men[98] continue to be compelled by God's grace and the empowerment of the Holy Spirit[99].

We affirm the theological approach of the Lausanne Movement's Cape Town Commitment as a foundation for our Call to all Christians:

> "That all of us, men and women, married and single are responsible to employ God's gifts for the benefit of others as stewards of God's grace and for the praise and glory of Christ. [We] are also responsible to enable all God's people to exercise all the gifts that God has given for all the areas of service to which God calls the Church."[100]

We are compelled, building on this Biblical foundation, to broaden our awareness, increase our attentiveness, and commit to specific actions to restore God's intention for all people.

AWARENESS

We recognise that our communities and leadership structures have not always been encouraging, freeing or even safe for women and girls, who are each valued and loved by God.

We acknowledge that the pathways for women to serve as leaders in the global Church are limited, and this has prevented many from contributing to the Church in this way.

---

[96] The Call to All Christians is available in 10 languages at https://www.riseinstrength.net/download-the-call.
[97] (John 10:10b).
[98] (Gen 1:26-8; 2:23).
[99] (Acts 1:8).
[100] https://www.lausanne.org/content/ctc/ctcommitment#capetown, p.6.

We acknowledge that the Church has deeply hurt many women and girls, and not heard or acknowledged their pain.

We acknowledge that violence, in all its forms, towards women is perpetrated not only outside the Church, but also inside.

ATTENTIVENESS

We **recognize** that the global Church has too often ignored the voices of women in its communities.

We commit to being attentive to these voices, including experiences, perspectives, joys and suffering.

We commit to being attentive to women and girls among the most vulnerable populations and regions of the world, especially those living in extreme poverty, or with disability, those endangered by human trafficking, persecuted for their faith, denied education and legal rights – and so at greatest risk of gender-based violence and discrimination.

We commit to discerning the spiritual gifts of all women and girls, so as to draw upon resources God has given for the full health and strength of the whole Church, wherever it manifests across every sector of our society.

ACTION

We must all act to:

Engage in a positive dialogue, mourning and repenting of mistakes and the pain we have caused, and seeking reconciliation; believing this is a first step to making our communities more empowered in Christ and safer places for women, girls, men and boys.

Celebrate the strength, courage, gifts and work of women in churches around the globe.

Work in unity to address the issues which concern us regarding the most vulnerable populations, especially those in extreme poverty and facing persecution for their faith.

Consecrate our gifts and opportunities to further strengthen, grow and mature our local churches and the global Church, in imitation of Christ's example of Servant leadership.

Commit to collaboration between women and men.[101]

Equip women and girls to take up leadership positions in the Church and wider society, including training and development, making the most of innovative resources.

We call on men and women of the global Church to act so that women, men, girls and boys can all embrace their spiritual giftings to strengthen the work of the Church, and Her witness to the glory of God.

---

[101] Eph 5:21, John 17:21-3.

Other Resources

This list of resources is wide-ranging in approach (but certainly not exhaustive) and we hope that something sparks your interest as you explore, learn and ponder.

Plight of women

Christine Schirrmacher and Thomas Schirrmacher, **The Oppression of Women: Violence – Exploitation – Poverty**, 2020, Verlag für Kultur und Wissenschaft.

Open Doors International, **The Hidden Face of Persecution,** 2020, https://media.opendoorsuk.org/document/pdf/2020-The-Hidden-Face-of-Persecution.pdf.

Peirong Lin (Ed.), **Gender and Religious Freedom**, International Journal for Religious Freedom, 2016, https://iirf.eu/journal-books/iirf-journal/ijrf-vol-9-issue-1-2-2016/.

Women as co-workers and co-leaders

Katia Adams, **Equal: What the Bible Says about Women, Men and Authority**, 2019, David C Cook.

Loren Cunningham and David Joel Hamilton, **Why Not Women: A Fresh Look at Scripture on Women in Missions, Ministry and Leadership**, 2000, YWAM Publishing.

Grady J Lee, **10 Lies the Church Tells Women: How the Bible has been Misused to keep Women in Spiritual Bondage**, revised 2006, Charisma House.

Rosemary Dewerse and Cathy Hine, **"Reading from Worlds under the Text: Oceanic Women in the Missio Dei"** in Mission Studies 37 (2020), Issue 1, Journal of the International Association for Mission Studies. Koninklijke Brill NV, Leiden, 2020.

Lynne Hybels, **Nice Girls don't Change the World**, 2005, Zondervan.

Amanda Jackson and Trina Simpson, **Wake Up, Rise in Strength**, 2017 women.worldea.org/training-for-women.

Carolyn Custis James, **Half the Church: Recapturing God's Global Vision for Women**, 2010, Zondervan.

Nicholas D Kristof and Sheryl Wudunn, **Half the Sky: How to Change the World,** 2009, Virago.

Ksenija Magda, **Blessing the Curse: A Biblical Approach for Restoring Relationships in the Church**, 2020, Langham Global Library.

Florence Muindi, **The Pursuit of His Calling,** 2008, Integrity Publishers.

WEA Women's Commission and CNEDA, **A Christian View of Relationships to End Domestic Abuse**, 2020, https://www.evoj.org/books-guides

Women in the Bible

Andrew Bartlett, **Men and Women in Christ: Fresh Light from the Biblical Texts**, 2019, Inter Varsity Press.

Mary J Evans, **Woman in the Bible: An Overview of All the Crucial Passages on Women's Roles,** 1984, IVP.

Lindsay Hardin Freeman, **Bible Women: All Their Words and Why They Matter**, 2014, Forward Movement.

Sandra Glahn (ed), **Vindicating the Vixens: Revisiting Sexualised, Vilified and Marginalised Women of the Bible**, 2017, Kregel.

Lucy Peppiatt, **Rediscovering Scripture's Vision for Women: Fresh Perspectives on Disputed Texts**, 2019, Inter Varsity Press.

Women in personal relationships

Elizabeth Beyer, **Mutual by Design: A Better Model of Christian Marriage**, 2017, CBE International.

Tim and Anne Evans, **Together: Reclaiming Co-Leadership in Marriage**, 2014, Real Life Ministries USA.

Rachel Held Evans, **A Year of Biblical Womanhood**, 2012, Thomas Nelson.

The **Marriage Preparation** and **Marriage** courses devised by HTB Church in London, are designed to help couples discuss all sorts of marriage issues. Feedback is provided on the assessments they complete. Many non-Christian couples do the courses. See https://www.htb.org/premarriage and https://themarriagecourse.org.

Prepare Enrich is an online relationship inventory and skill-building program that provides couples exercises to build their relationship skills.

Based on a couple's assessment results, a trained facilitator provides 3 or more feedback sessions to help the couple discuss and understand their results. See their website https://www.prepare-enrich.eu/en/

Blogs that cover gender issues and social issues impacting women

Amanda Jackson covers social issues, church and the public sphere from a woman's perspective. Her blog is **Amandaadvocates.**

Dr Claude Mariottini is Emeritus Professor of Old Testament at Northern Baptist Seminary in the USA. He blogs on the Hebrew Bible from a Christian perspective and has many articles on Bible women. His blog is **Claude Mariottini.**

Other Resources

Dr Nijay K. Gupta is a theologian and New Testament scholar. His blog, **Crux Sola**, is subtitled "Formed by Scripture to Live Like Christ." Nijay is writing a book about New Testament women which will be published by IVP Academic.

Marg Mowczko's blogsite, **Marg Mowczko**, explores the biblical theology of Christian egalitarianism. Her blogs and articles cover a wide range of subjects with erudite precision and she also makes helpful recommendations on other writers.

Various writers contribute to the blog, **Theological Miscellany**, by the faculty and friends of Westminster Theological College in the UK. They post theological reflections on scripture, life, culture, politics, society and gender.

Many blog posts are written by Dr Lucy Peppiatt (see her book above).

Scripture Index

Genesis
- 1 98
- 1:26 41
- 1:26-28 26
- 1:26-8 141
- 1:27 . 37, 39, 48, 80, 97
- 1:27.31 39
- 1:27-28 75
- 2 .... 40, 71
- 2:20–23 37
- 2:21 77
- 2:23 141
- 2:20b-23 27
- 3 71
- 3:1–24 37
- 3:16 28
- 11:30 29
- 11:31 28
- 11:42 79
- 12:15–16 29
- 12:4 28
- 12:10 28
- 12:13 28
- 12:15 29
- 12:17 29
- 16 114
- 16:2 29
- 16:4 29
- 16:6 29
- 17:18 22
- 20:3 29
- 20:12 28
- 20:13 29
- 21:9 29
- 21:10 29

Judges
- 4 76
- 4:4 76
- 13 21

Ruth
- 1:1 30
- 1:2 29
- 1:3 29
- 1:4-5 29
- 1:11 29
- 2:2 30
- 2:8-9 30
- 2:22 30
- 3:1 30
- 3:4 30
- 4:1-10 30

1. Samuel
- 16:7 98

2. Samuel
- 13 22
- 20 75

2. Kings
- 22 19

1. Chronicles
- 7:24 75

Psalms
- 33:20 27
- 70:5 27
- 115:9 27
- 133:1 96
- 139:13 128
- 139:14 127

Proverbs
- 31 21

Ecclesiastes
- 4:8 91
- 4:9-10 91

Isaiah
- 6:3 99
- 61:10 40

Jeremiah
- 17:9 127
- 17:10 128

Daniel
- 3:17-18 114

Matthew
- 5:3 32
- 5:5.38-48 85
- 6:26 26
- 9:9 14
- 12:49 50
- 15:23 51
- 18:19 92
- 19:1–12 43
- 20:25-26 93
- 23:14 83
- 23:23b 129
- 26 54
- 26:6-13 54
- 27:55-56 59
- 28 98

Mark
- 1:15 30
- 10:42-44 63
- 10:42-45 85
- 12:43 48
- 14 54
- 14:3-9 54
- 15:40-41 59

Luke
- 1:49 49
- 1:51-53 49
- 4:18-19 48

4:21 48	1:13-14 60	16:3-16 65
5:26 14	1:15 .... 57, 60	16:3-5a 66
5:30-31 14	2:16–18 42	16:3-5 66
7 54	2:17-18 .... 60, 75	16:4 69
8:1-3 .... 59, 121	2:33 75	16:6 69
8:3 53	2:46 61	16:6.12 69
8:48 47	5:42 61	16:7 .... 69, 75, 76
10 .... 16, 53	6 61	16:9 66
10:1 92	8:3 .... 69, 75	16:21 66
10:2 31	8:27 82	16:3–7 37
10:38-42 53	9:36-42 62	
10:39-40 121	9:1ff 69	**1. Corinthians**
17:17-19 47	12 61	1:12 70
17:21 30	14:3-4.14 70	2:16 135
18:8 136	16:14 62	3:5 63
22:24-27 63	16:40 62	3:8 68
22:27 63	17:25 99	4:1 63
23:28 56	18:2.18.26 66	4:12 68
	18:24-26 66	7 72
John	18:26 .... 66, 76, 77	7:39 83
2:5 50	21:9 .... 62, 76	11:2–16 35
4 51	22:4 69	11:1 .... 85, 135
4:1-26 43	25:13 82	11:5 .... 43, 65
4:18 52		11:7–9 .... 37, 40
4:26 .... 51, 122	**Romans**	12 .... 42, 72
4:29 52	3:23 27	12:12–20 43
4:32-33 52	5:11 129	12:1-11 76
4:39 51	7:21-24 128	12:4-11 75
8:3-11 43	7:25a 128	12:5 83
8:3-11 48	8:18 33	12:12-31ff 133
10:10b 141	8:29 85	12:13 135
11 53	12:2a 135	12:26 32
11:1-44 53	12:1-2 .... 131, 132	12:4–7.11 42
12 54	12:1-8 76	12-14 39
12:3 54	12:2 135	13:4b-7 138
13:3-15 63	12:6-8 72	13:4-7 138
14:6 99	12:8 69	14:26 65
17:18-26 130	12:14-21 85	14:26-40 65
17:20 133	12:4–5.16 43	14:26-40 72
17:21 .... 95, 130	13:1-5 63	14:34 .... 40, 78
17:21-3 143	13:4 63	14:34-35 72
17:23 97	13:8 134	15:10 68
19: 26-27 49	15:8 63	16:16 .... 68, 69
20:21 130	15:25 63	16:19 66
	16 .... 15, 72	
Acts	16:1-2 .... 63, 64	**2. Corinthians**
1:8 141	16:2 67	5:14a 134

Scripture Index

5:16-18 133
5:17 85
6:1 134
6:4 63
8:23 .... 67, 70
11:13-15 63

Galatians
1:6–7 38
2:17 63
3:26–27 38
3:18 133
3:24 38
3:26-28 85
3:26-29 75
3:28 ..... 35, 38, 83, 135
4:11 68
4:1–7 38
5:13-14 85
5:22-23 138
5:2–3.12 38
6:11–15 38
6:15 42

Ephesians
3:7 63
4:2-3 132
4:4 83
4:6-13 76
4:11-13 72
5:22–23 37
5:2 85
5:21 143
5:23 81
5:31 83
6:21-22 63

Philippians
2:1-4 68
2:1-8 32
2:2 68

2: 5-11 132
2:5 68
2:16 68
2:25 .... 67, 70
3:4-7 47
3:20-21 47
4:2-3 .... 67, 70

Colossians
1:7 63
1:23 63
1:29 68
3:11 135
3:15 43
3:16 .... 65, 83
4:7-9 63
4:10-11 67
4:15 70

1. Thessalonians
1:1 70
2:6 70
2:9 68
3:5 68
5:12 69
5:12-13 69

2. Thessalonians
3:8 68

1. Timothy
1:3-4.7 71
2:11–15 .... 35, 43
2:8–15 37
2:12–14 41
2:8 71
2:8-15 72
2:9-10 71
2:11-15 .... 59, 71, 81
2:12 .... 40, 59, 71, 76
2:13 .... 77, 80

2:13-14 71
2:15 71
3:1-7 61
3:4.5.12 69
4:3a 71
4:6 63
5:2 138
5:17 .... 68, 69

2. Timothy
4 15
4:19 66

Titus
2:4–5 43
3:8.14 69

Philemon
1 67
24 67

Hebrews
2-10 75

James
1:2 132

1. Peter
1:15-16 99
2:9 .... 75, 131
3:9 85

1. John
3:2 85
4:16b-18a 138

2. John
1:10 61

Revelation
1:6 75
5:10 75

Biographies

Andrew Bartlett, QC, is based in London and is a highly rated international arbitrator with a wide range of experience in dispute resolution in numerous locations from North America to the Far East. In addition, he has a BA in Theology (University of Gloucestershire) and has served as an elder and a churchwarden in various churches. Andrew is married, with three children and five grandchildren. He is the author of Men and Women in Christ: Fresh Light from the Biblical Texts.

Emma Dipper, from the UK, is Founding Director of Gender and Religious Freedom and is on the leadership team of the WEA Women's Commission. She teaches at All Nations Christian College on a theology of suffering, persecution and mission. She trained and worked as a nurse and midwife. **Andy** is Principal and CEO of All Nations Christian College, UK. An engineer by background, he has worked in the UK and in international development. They have three daughters.

Mary Evans (PhD) is a former theological lecturer who is still involved with research supervision and marking. Writing, speaking, church, family, friends and Langham Partnership Board responsibilities fill much of the rest of available time. Her books include 1 and 2 Samuel in the Bible Speaks today series, and the Tyndale commentary on Judges and Ruth.

Rosalee Velloso Ewell (PhD) is a theologian from São Paulo, Brazil. She has served as Executive Director of the Theological Commission of the World Evangelical Alliance as a volunteer. Rosalee is also Director of Church Relations for the United Bible Societies and the author or editor of various books and articles. She currently lives in the U.K. with her family.

Alison Guinness is a missionary who has been working with the Church in Burundi since 2009. She works on developing new opportunities to help send Burundian missionaries to work in North Africa. Alison met Paul Guinness in Burundi and they were married in 2015. Baby Jeremy joined the family a year later and was followed by Grace in 2018 and Lydia in 2020.

Amanda Jackson is the Director of the Women's Commission of the WEA. She is one of the founders of Rise in Strength, a network of international Christian women leaders. She is the Chair of Kyria Network and facilitates the Christian Network to End Domestic Abuse. Born in Australia, Amanda has lived in the UK for many years. She is married and has two wonderful adult children.

Peirong Lin (PhD) originally from Singapore, currently lives in Bonn, Germany. She is the Deputy Secretary General for Operations of the World Evangelical Alliance (WEA). She is passionate about theology influencing everyday life. She is an affiliated researcher of North-West University South Africa and the Evangelische Theologische Faculteit, Leuven, Belgium. She is married and has one toddling son.

Jay Matenga (PhD) identifies as a New Zealand Māori and lives in Auckland New Zealand. He leads Missions Interlink NZ, the missions alliance of New Zealand, and is Director of Missions and Evangelism for the WEA, a responsibility of which is leading the WEA's Mission Commission. Jay has a passion for promoting mutuality as mission, a concept that he developed for his doctorate from Fuller School of Intercultural Studies.

Margaret Mowczko is an Australian theologian and writer. Her area of interest is the mutuality (equality) of men and women in Christian ministry and marriage. Margaret has a BTh from the Australian College of Ministries and an MA in early Christian and Jewish studies from Macquarie University. She blogs at MargMowczko.com

Dr. **Florence Muindi**, based in Kenya, is the Founder President and CEO of Life in Abundance International (LIA). She oversees community development work in 12 countries in Africa, two in the Caribbean. She is a medical doctor specialising in public health, a mother, author, speaker and an ordained minister. She and her husband, Dr. Festus, have been cross cultural missionaries for 25 years.

Samuel O. Okanlawon (PhD) is a Senior Lecturer in the Department of Religious Studies, University of Ibadan, Nigeria. His area of specialisation is Christian Theology. He pastors a local church congregation in Ibadan. Also, he conducts Leadership Development classes in public secondary schools in Ibadan and is a social commentator on ecclesial and national issues on both traditional and online media channels. He is the Editor of the Nigerian Association for Christian Studies that publishes the *Nigerian Journal of Christian Studies* and a member of the Editorial Board of the *International Journal of Religion and Traditions* (Ghana).

Evi Rodemann, from Germany, is a theologian and event manager. She is passionate about young people and in various leadership roles connects and develops younger leaders globally. She has an MA in European Mission (UK) and studies for a PhD in Missiology (UNISA).

Reverends **Gabriel & Jeanette Salguero** are co-lead pastors of The Gathering Place in Orlando, Florida, and founders of The National Latino Evangelical Coalition. They are proud parents of Jon-Gabriel & Seth Salguero. Together, they minister locally & globally focusing on Gospel-centred transformation for the common good.

Madleine Sara is a professor and counselor at Bethlehem Bible College. She also provides pastoral ministry in the Jerusalem Alliance Church, where she preaches and is part of the pastoral team. As a mentor to many emerging Arab women leaders and theologians, she edits and writes for a women's magazine that she publishes called 'Anyeh biyadeh' which is translated to a pot in His hand. She is married to Jack Sara and together they have three children.

Leslie and Chad Neal Segraves, from the USA, have lived for many years in Asia as mission directors of 10/40 Connections which they founded in 2000, to spread tangible hope to unreached peoples. They are speakers, authors, and parents of four children. They recently began Life Voices, a network of believers seeking to advance the culture of life and stop the global genocide of abortion. Both have PhDs in Missiology from Fuller. They serve as co- catalysts for Women and Men Partnering in the Gospel with the Lausanne Movement.

Amy Summerfield is a speaker and leadership advisor in the UK. She is CEO of Kyria Network and Head of Development for Skylark International, a church network. When she's not busy speaking, blogging and leading the Kyria team, she loves drinking tea, cooking, dog walking and film watching.

Menchit Wong from the Philippines, has over 30 years' experience in international Christian ministries, including the Lausanne Movement International Board, Global Children's Forum Strategy Team and World Without Orphans Leadership Council.